2S

C0-AVX-806

STRAIGHT
FROM THE
SHOULDER

REV. THOMAS J. HOSTY, M.A., S.T.B.

Preface by
THE RIGHT REV. DANIEL F. CUNNINGHAM
Superintendent of Schools, Archdiocese of Chicago

PURCELL HIGH SCHOOL LIBRARY
2935 HACKBERRY STREET
CINCINNATI 6, OHIO

THE BRUCE PUBLISHING COMPANY
MILWAUKEE

NIHIL OBSTAT: J. J. CLIFFORD, S.J.
IMPRIMATUR: SAMUEL ALPHONSUS STRITCH,
ARCHIEPISCOPUS CHICAGOENSIS
NOVEMBER 11, 1944

242
H

COPYRIGHT, 1946, BY
THE BRUCE PUBLISHING COMPANY
PRINTED IN THE U. S. A.

7055 Benz 10/46 1.50

THIS BOOK IS LOVINGLY DEDICATED

TO

MY SAINTLY MOTHER,

WHO TAUGHT HER NINE CHILDREN

"STRAIGHT FROM THE HEART,"

WHAT I AM TRYING TO WRITE

"STRAIGHT FROM THE SHOULDER."

PREFACE

ONE of the most difficult tasks in the priest's preaching ministry is to by-pass, as far as possible, the theological verbiage which is necessarily connected with the imparting of God's word, so that His hearers may adequately grasp the underlying significance of divine truth. "Only recently," a distinguished Catholic layman confessed, "have I acquired the power to look beyond the mere words of the Scriptures to the deep reality of the Gospel message, and the fuller understanding of that message has had a profound influence on my life." The priest's task in this respect is admittedly more difficult when he is attempting to unfold God's truth to the young.

The author of this series of talks to young men and women of high-school and college age has been eminently successful in this regard. Father Hosty knows young people. He knows their problems, he speaks their language, and he has that all too rare gift of being able to adapt the language and idioms of modern youth to religious instruction. The fruit of his method has been to deepen religious conviction in the minds of young people and to hearten them in the pursuit of virtue and truth.

The outstanding success of his retreats to high-

school and college groups has been widely acclaimed
by school principals and students alike. In the hope
of influencing still more students these talks are pre-
sented here in book form, and this book in the hands
of high-school and college students will prove a valu-
able addition to the religion course of study.

DANIEL F. CUNNINGHAM

FOREWORD

BEWARE of the man who writes one book!" I had heard that phrase many times but never realized its full meaning — until my first book was published. Now I know. Believe me, all the literary travail that went with delivering my first-born printed effort was speedily forgotten, in the joy that was mine as an author. Though I live to be a thousand, I shall never forget the thrill of gazing for the first time upon my academic offspring, anemic and thin-covered as it was. But my triumph proved to be short-lived. Soon my friends began to ask: "When is your next book coming out?" At first I was able to laugh off their queries, or dismiss them with a knowing shrug. When a year had elapsed, however, and there was still no sign of any renewed literary effort on my part, my friends (what few there were left) began to favor me with an icy stare. I could have stood that, but it was their unspoken though oft-implied taunt that finally got the better of me: "He quit writing, because he hasn't anything else worth while to say. We wouldn't mind so much, if he hadn't 'needled' us so unmercifully in the foreword of his first book. The fact that 'even the great Homer nods' is no excuse for this fourth-rate Virgil to go into perpetual hibernation."

To still the voice of questioning critics, and because I sincerely believe I have something worth while for young people to hear, I have again thrown my hat into the literary ring. As in my first book, so here do I humbly disclaim any great originality. Probably, the one attractive feature of this book will be the fact that it is written in the "straight from the shoulder" manner that young people of high-school and college age delight in employing.

The entire book has been built around the idea of heaven, the end and object of all our earthly endeavors. However, it begins, not on a heavenly theme, but with a deliberately provocative attack upon those who listen to and read books of this sort, without profiting in the least. The second chapter is concerned with heaven itself. The next three chapters deal with the great hurdles on the obstacle course to heaven, the practice of the virtues of purity and charity. Then, logically, the following four chapters treat of the four great helps along the road to heaven — Prayer, Confession, Holy Communion, and the Mass. Since there are only four possible roads to heaven, the next chapter discusses these roads under the more common name, Vocation. The concluding chapter, as would be expected, is dedicated to an inspirational talk on Christ, our Lord — our model, our hero, and our inspiration, on the road to heaven.

If it should seem presumptuous to offer this book to young people, my one extenuating plea is this: I admire them so much that I am willing to brave any kind of criticism to try to help them.

All of the talks in this book have been delivered a number of times, on the occasion of high-school and college retreats. At least, therefore, they have been submitted to some sort of practical test. That they may prove helpful, at least in some small degree, to our young people, is the sincere hope and prayer of the writer and preacher of these pages.

FATHER TOM HOSTY

CONTENTS

Chapter 1

READ THIS FIRST

WHAT effect do sermons have upon you? In view of the fact that you've heard hundreds of them in your lifetime, and are going to read more of them here, that is not only a fair question, but also a very important one. But there is another reason for asking that question. Ever since we were youngsters, we've heard people discussing the sermons of various priests, generally in a dissatisfied tone of voice. Since my ordination, I've heard the subject even more. It seems to be the great American Catholic pastime. To hear some people talk, you'd think the sermon was a sort of spiritual dessert, to be completely enjoyed by one and all; that it was a literary or rhetorical dumpling into which every parishioner was invited to stick his critical fork, and praise or blame the cook.

The desire to correct that attitude is the purpose of this chapter. If you're going to wade through the others that follow, you really ought to try to get something out of them. How seldom have I heard anyone say that a particular sermon had influenced his life in any

1

way! Yet, that is the real test of a good sermon, for sermons are delivered (either orally or through the medium of print) not merely to be liked, but to be *lived*. The way to judge a sermon is to measure its effect upon your life and conduct.

When I started in the seminary, I learned that lesson from a saintly old professor. A well-known Jesuit had preached our first retreat. Shortly after the retreat was over, I was out walking and bumped into this old professor. In the course of our conversation, I mentioned the wonderful retreat we had just made. The professor smiled at my youthful enthusiasm; then he said, "I'll tell you how good your retreat was, six months from now."

That same lesson was brought home to me even more clearly about nine years ago. The occasion was a novena service in honor of Our Lady of Perpetual Help. The incident happened when I was a curate, shortly after my first appointment. In my sermon, at the novena devotion, I stressed the idea that the real way to make the novena would be to complete the prayers by receiving Holy Communion every Tuesday morning in honor of Our Lady. In typical blushing-violet style, I felt that it was a fairly good talk. As a matter of fact, there were a few compliments on it which I was still young and callow enough to swallow. I went to bed that night, serene in the expectation that the next day would mark a new record for the number of those receiving daily Communion in that parish.

In fact, I even seriously contemplated asking the other curate to help me give Holy Communion the next morning. On second thought, I decided to wait until it was his turn to celebrate the early Mass, and then surprise him with the crowd. When I turned around to give the blessing before distributing Holy Communion that next morning, I swallowed one of the bitterest pills in my young lifetime. There was not a single *new* person at the Communion rail!

Why have the sermons you have heard or read produced little or no effect upon you? Probably the one big objection in the back of your mind is this: "The reason we don't get anything out of the sermons is that they are no good!" What shall I say to that?

Granting, merely for the sake of argument, that the sermon is often dull, tiresome, and pointless; even conceding that it might merit the caustic rebuke of a pastor to his newly ordained assistant that there were only three things wrong with his first sermon — "it was not well prepared; it was not well delivered; and it was not worth preparing"; even conceding all this, still I say that it is your own fault, if you don't get anything out of a sermon. For proof, there is the example of Saint Francis Xavier, probably the greatest missionary that the Church has had since Saint Paul.

When Francis was a young man, at the University of Paris, his future promised to be very brilliant because of his remarkable talents. One day he met a fellow Spaniard by the name of Ignatius. This young Spaniard was then engaged in trying to organize the society that was later to become one of the great orders in the Catholic Church — the Jesuits. Ignatius was struck by the genius of the youthful collegian and tried to get him to join his Society. Everything Ignatius said, to induce Francis to give up a worldly career, fell upon deaf ears, with the exception of one sentence: "What does it profit a man if he gains the whole world and suffers the loss of his own soul?" In other words, the only thing that Francis got out of all Ignatius' preaching was one single thought; yet, that one thought was the reason why Francis Xavier became a saint, and ultimately lead over a million souls to the feet of their crucified Master.

No matter how poor a sermon may seem to you, there is always something you can get out of it, even if it's only a prayer for the preacher. Therefore, I have some accusations to make on this point. It will be up to your own conscience to plead guilty to the accusation that strikes home. If you are guilty, make an honest effort to correct your viewpoint, so that you'll get everything possible out of the rest of this book.

First, there are some who are *too proud* to profit by any sermon. What the priest says about their favorite vice may be true; nevertheless, they resent it. "Who does he think he is, anyway, talking down to us, as though we were still a bunch of grammar school kids? You'd think he was a saint himself, to hear him talk!"

To those afflicted with that spiritual disease, I say that the preacher does not pose as a paragon of all virtues, although, if he is sincere, he should be trying to practice what he preaches. But, he is fulfilling a solemn obligation, imposed upon him by Christ Himself, to feed His lambs with the bread of truth. A priest who knows the faults of his congregation, and then deliberately refrains from condemning those faults, is a coward and a traitor to his divine calling. It is true that he may not be perfect himself. Please remember that only God is perfect.

Second, there are those who are *too indifferent* — the "So what!" type — to profit by a sermon. A sermon doesn't impress them one way or another, providing it isn't too long. For all they care, or for all the mental attention they give him, the priest might just as well be reciting the alphabet or a multiplication table. If the priest were ever to interrupt his talk, and offer them the proverbial "penny for their thoughts," he would lose money on the deal. For this type of person, the best sermon is no sermon.

The third class embraces all those who are *self-satisfied*. They realize that everything the priest says is true; but, after all, they feel that they could be a whole lot worse. Oh, they'll admit that they drink a little too much, every now and then, and that they are not too scrupulous about getting to Mass on time, or observing the Church's laws on fasting and abstinence; and, as for getting to Communion regularly on

Sunday — well, it's a grand thing, but it interferes with Saturday night. Their attitude could probably be summed up in this way: "Father has to preach every Sunday. I have to listen every Sunday. He does his part. I do my part. Perhaps I don't do everything that he teaches or pay too much attention to what he says, but if he were in my circumstances, he probably wouldn't either." I only hope the Lord will not be too hard on people of that kind.

The fourth group are the *emotional type*. They regard the sermon merely as a dessert, a spiritual luxury to be enjoyed to the utmost, but not to be acted upon. They remind me of the old lady that came home from church and went into ecstasies over the wonderful sermon the priest had delivered. Upon being questioned by her grandson as to the nature of the sermon, she couldn't remember a single word. "But, mind you, it was grand," she kept protesting.

People of this type sit back very contentedly in the pew and try to enjoy every minute of the talk — even the announcements! For them, the priest is a sort of ecclesiastical "master of ceremonies." It's the equivalent of going to a movie, where you don't have to do any thinking, but just relax and let the camera do the work. When the sermon is over, so are the images which it aroused in their imaginations, never, never, to return again. I think that a good many of us are in this class. We'll never know the joy we missed by not trying to put those sermons into action. Our spiritually barren, fruitless, monotonous lives will be our own punishment.

The fifth type are the *"money gripers."* They're always complaining that the priest never talks about anything but money. Generally, that is about the only reaction they do show to the talk, because invariably the ones who cry the loudest are the ones who give the least. It is true that in an exceptional case you find a priest who preaches too much about money, but one priest is not the whole Church. It certainly is true that from time to time it is necessary to remind the people of their solemn obligation to support the Church, according to their means. Believe me, priests don't relish that job, but, until the time when we can talk our creditors into taking prayers instead of cash in payment for church debts, they'll have to resign themselves to asking occasionally.

The sixth type are the *would-be intelligentsia,* the "cliché conscious" crowd. They listen to every sermon in a very critical frame of mind, ready to pounce upon the slightest mistake. Then they bravely discuss it at home, over a card table, or in some cocktail lounge, where, of course, the poor priest has no chance whatsoever of defending his views. They're generally younger people, who have been exposed to a fair education, who brag about the fact that the priests may be able to string along the old folks, but he isn't fooling them! No, sir! They went to a university and they read books and magazines. "The trouble with the sermons," they will say, "is that they are below our intellectual level." I remember a fairly prominent Catholic, from a swanky suburb, who decried the fact that the missionaries at his parish did not realize that his audience was of a more advanced intellectual level than the ordinary Catholic parishioner, with the result that they only preached on such common and time-worn subjects as heaven, hell, mortal sin, and the like! People with this frame of mind have as much chance of getting something out of a sermon as I have of being elected Emperor of Japan. Even heaven might prove to be a letdown for this type, I'm afraid.

Last, but far from least — in their own estimation! — are those who are afflicted with a sense of *self-righteousness*. Without the slightest effort on their part, they can apply every point in the sermon to someone whom they know. You can almost hear them saying right now: "I hope Mrs. So and So reads this book. Everything Father has said, so far, fits her to a T." What a shock this type will get on judgment day, when they discover that in searching for the mote in their neighbor's eye, they had overlooked the beam in their own!

Please remember that, if the priest has the duty of preaching (and writing) as well as he can, you have a corresponding obligation of hearing (and reading) and carrying out his sermons to the best of your ability. The next time you are tempted to criticize a sermon (probably right now, as soon as you finish this introduction), ask yourself, first, if you have made one single effort to profit by it. After all, it was to you that our Lord said, "Blessed are they who hear the word of God and keep it!"

Chapter 2

THE SIXTY-FOUR DOLLAR QUESTION AND ITS ANSWER

NEWSPAPERS often contain strange articles. I'm not referring to columns like Ripley's "Believe It or Not," but to everyday news items. One of the strangest and saddest examples of this fact may be found, frequently, tucked away in the corner of about the seventh or eighth page. Doctors call it amnesia, but we're familiar with it as a loss-of-memory case. One of them was reported in the daily paper just a few months ago. You probably read it, too. A well-dressed young man was being held for identification in a downtown police station. He had been wandering aimlessly around, in the business section. Upon being questioned by the police, he could not remember who he was. He could carry on a very intelligent conversation, but he could not tell his name, where he came from, or where he was going. I don't know what became of the poor fellow, and I never took the trouble to inquire. The point is that our sympathies are stirred up by his misfortune, our hearts go out to him. A sad case. But there are worse.

After all, that unfortunate young man was probably

regardless of whether, with my puny intellect, I can understand it or not, the fact of hell remains. Just as I may not be able to explain why the lights in a building are burning, although the fact remains that they are.

The second answer is a bit more disconcerting. God doesn't condemn me to hell; I condemn myself, if I go there. For example, the law of the state calls for the death penalty for the commission of certain crimes. Would you call the judge a monster of cruelty because he condemns a man, absolutely proven guilty of such a crime, to the electric chair? No — that criminal convicted himself. On judgment day, you will receive absolute justice. There won't be any crooked lawyers or sentimental juries to stay the verdict. And the fact that you may happen to be the only son of old John Money-Bags, or that you may have a pretty face, or that you may be related to some big politician, won't help you in the least.

The third answer is this: If the Second Person of the Blessed Trinity came down on earth and took upon Himself the nature of man so that He might undergo the excruciating agony of Calvary, to atone for sin, then mortal sin really must be a terrible thing and deserving of the greatest possible punishment. As a matter of record, God punished Lucifer and his followers forever, for one single serious sin.

In the last analysis, if there were no hell, there would be no justice. Hell is for the punishment of the injustice you see being done every day: old people, who saved all their lives to provide for their old age, being deprived of their just earnings by some crooked banker; fathers of families, underpaid by some greedy employer; small merchants, pushed to the wall by unscrupulous financiers; public works being drained dry by some money hungry politicians; young men dying on foreign fields because of power-obsessed dictators. All such things call to heaven for vengeance, and God will punish the guilty ones in hell.

We'll dismiss the subject of hell with this final thought: If the joys of heaven and the love of God ever fail to be sufficient motives to drive us from serious sin, then, please God, may the fear of hell do it.

With regard to heaven, it is my firm conviction that this joyful side of our religion is not sufficiently emphasized. There's too much talk about hell and too little about heaven. This life, at its best, is no bargain; hard work, sickness, worry, and heartaches are the common lot of all of us. And worst of all is the monotony of everyday existence. There may be a thrill to monotony for some people, but for me, variety is still the spice of life. We must try to soften these difficulties as much as possible by looking forward to the next life. Let's look forward to heaven as the boy in school looks forward to the summer vacation. If we can spend all year planning where we're going to go on our short vacation, we can give a great deal more thought to where we hope to spend our eternity.

A priest friend of mine who had been studying at Rome, went for a cruise, during the summer, on the Mediterranean Sea. On the boat, he made the acquaintance of a young archaeologist who had graduated from an American university. Sad to say he was an atheist — he did not believe in the existence of God. My priest friend and the archaeologist spent many pleasant moments together, discussing practically every subject imaginable. One afternoon, however, a remark was made that really set my friend thinking. They were lounging on deck chairs, watching the sun set over the placid waters of the blue Mediterranean — one of the most beautiful sights in the world. Suddenly, my priest friend remembered that he had not even begun to say his Office, and so, very reluctantly, he rose to his feet, and got ready to go to his cabin, to start his prayers. As he did, the young atheist looked at him very wistfully, and said, "I certainly envy you. You can afford to pass up this magnificent view, because your religion tells you (and I know that you believe it!) that, after death, you will see beauty that will make this sunset seem, by comparison, like the reflection of the sun in a muddy pool of water. But, for me, this is one of the supreme moments of life. I couldn't pass up this opportunity if I wanted to, because life is so short, and death will mean the end of everything for me."

Much as we might be inclined to pity that young

man, to a certain extent, we must admire him. At least
he acted consistently with his beliefs. On the other
hand, how often has the thought of heaven had any
practical bearing upon your life? Has it ever kept you
from committing a single serious sin? What is your
idea of heaven? If heaven is going to be a great
influence in your life, to help you persevere in the
service of God, you should have at least a few definite
ideas about it.

What is heaven, anyway? The best way to answer
that question is to begin by telling what it is not.
Heaven is not a place where we'll spend our time,
parked on pink clouds, strumming on a harp, and fan-
ning ourselves with palm branches — or winging our
way down golden streets, through pearly gates. That
is merely a poetic version of heaven.

And heaven isn't a place where we'll just sit around,
making a lot of pious talk. If heaven meant just one
long vacation, with absolutely nothing to do but listen
to a gathering of religious fanatics, talking about
things we didn't have the slightest interest in, you'd
be bored stiff in a week. You'd like anything better
than an eternity like that. And yet that is the idea some
people seem to have about heaven. No wonder the
thought of heaven hasn't been a very powerful motive
in our lives! No wonder some people prefer to go to
hell! They've got such a peculiar idea about heaven
that they believe that all the "live wires" will be down
in hell, and all the bead-rattling, "stick-in-the-mud,"

"8-o'clock crowd" will be in heaven. If heaven were like that, I wouldn't blame them. I think I'd rather go to hell myself. I certainly wouldn't want to be bored for all eternity.

But heaven isn't like that. Then, where in the world did people ever get such queer ideas about it? One explanation is the fact that people don't hear enough sermons giving a true picture of heaven.

Another source of misunderstanding is found in some of our prayers for the dead. We say: "Eternal *rest*, grant unto them, O Lord"; "May the souls of the faithful departed, through the mercy of God, *rest* in peace." A good many people, when they hear the word, *rest*, immediately think of sleep. They have the wrong idea about that word. It isn't synonymous with inactivity. It means merely a different kind of activity than we've been used to. For example, when you go away on a vacation, you go for a rest. That doesn't mean that you're not going to do a single thing but sleep. It simply means that, instead of doing things you're sick and tired of doing, you go out to fish, swim, play golf, play cards, dance, sleep late in the morning, and whatever else you might enjoy. When you come back from such a vacation, you tell everyone how grand it was and what a fine rest you had. Well, in heaven, you're going to rest for all eternity and be doing things far different from what you have to do on earth.

What is heaven actually like? It is a place that is better than all the kingdoms of the world. Recall to your minds the splendor of ancient Rome, the culture of Athens, the glories of Persia, and the wonders of our present civilization. Try to visualize all these rolled into one, and then listen to the words of Christ: "What does it profit a man if he gains the whole world and suffers the loss of his own soul?" In other words, it would be better to lose the whole world, with all its riches, than it would be to lose heaven.

Or let us suppose that you think of all the beautiful things you have seen in your lifetime; then recall all the wonderful places you have heard or read about; then try to imagine the most marvelous sights you can. Combine all these things, and you still haven't even a faint idea of what heaven is really like. How do we know that? Because the divinely inspired St. Paul said so. "Eye hath not seen, nor ear heard, neither hath it entered into the heart of man, what things God has prepared for those who love Him" (1 Cor. 2:9).

Heaven is the face-to-face sight of God Himself. In that vision, all our faculties will be perfectly satisfied. Have you ever been thrilled, on a beautiful spring morning, by the sheer joy of being alive? Don't you like to be on the "go"? It's a sure sign that you're growing old, when you start losing your pep. Well, heaven will be the land of eternal youth, because, in heaven, we'll possess the source of all life and energy, the First Person of the Most Blessed Trinity, God the Father.

We all like to know things. There is some curiosity in all of us. Millions of dollars are spent every year on books, and magazines, and travel, just to satisfy that mental instinct that is so deep in all of us. In heaven, there will never be a dull moment, because we'll be learning something new every minute. Why? Because we'll have before us, for our eternal contemplation, the source of all truth, God the Son, the Second Person of the Blessed Trinity.

Our hearts, which were made for love, will finally be satisfied, because they will be united forever with the great lover, the source of all true love, love personified, God the Holy Ghost, the Third Person of the Blessed Trinity.

The various senses of our body, too, will be given perfect satisfaction. No more sickness, no more suffering, no more pain, no more sorrow, forever, and ever, and ever. What a glorious prospect! Best of all, it is within the grasp of every one of us!

Almighty God offers heaven to those who persevere in their love for Him. What are a few short years of suffering, compared to an eternity of perfect happiness? What a fool I would be to barter away the unspeakable joys of heaven for a few years of earthly pleasure!

God is waiting for every one of us, at the end of the road of life, to bestow upon us a happiness that is simply indescribable, provided we prove, by our life and actions here below, that we really love Him. God grant that every one of us may receive the gift of final perseverance, so that, as eternity hangs in the balance, we may be able to hear with a joyful and expectant heart the solemn words of the priest who anoints us: "Depart, O Christian soul, out of this sinful world, in the name of God, the Father Almighty, who created thee; in the name of Jesus Christ, the Son of the living God, who suffered and died for thee; in the name of the Holy Ghost, who sanctified thee."

Chapter 3

WHAT PRICE GLORY?

THE purpose of our life, the reason that we exist, is to serve God. If we serve God faithfully during the span of life that is allotted to us, some time after death, we shall be rewarded with the everlasting possession of heaven, a place of unbelievable happiness and joy. On the other hand, if we deliberately fail to serve God, we shall be punished forever in a place called hell.

It is time now to consider what is undoubtedly one of the greatest obstacles on the road to heaven. If you were to take up a straw vote among all the Christians in the world over fourteen years of age, to determine the most difficult commandment of God, the overwhelming response would be: The sixth commandment. The sixth commandment, of course, is concerned with the exercise of the virtue of purity. If you never have any difficulties with regard to the virtue of purity, then I say that you are most unusual. Do you know why I say that? And, why I say that the virtue of purity is such a difficult one? — Because hand in hand with the practice of purity goes the instinct of race preservation, or, as it is more commonly called, the sex instinct. Next to the instinct of self-preservation, the strongest instinct that we have is the urge to perpetuate ourselves, to keep the human race going. Every normal human being has those instincts. They are part of God's plan of life.

The first three chapters of the Bible explain very clearly the plan of life laid down by Almighty God. Through the mutual co-operation of man and woman, this earth of ours was and is to be populated. This co-operation is to be a permanent affair, based upon a natural contract called marriage. So important did Jesus Christ, our Saviour, consider this contract that He raised it to the dignity of a sacrament. And, since marriage is the state in life to which the majority of you will be called and since marriage is so intimately bound up with the virtue of purity, it is absolutely imperative that you have a few clear ideas with regard to it.

Marriage entails many responsibilities and demands many sacrifices. For both men and women, it calls for readjustments and sacrifices known only to themselves and to Almighty God. God anticipated those difficulties, and so, in addition to the almost innumerable graces that He grants, by virtue of the sacramental character of matrimony, He also plants deep in the heart of every sincerely married couple a marvelous bond of love. That love expresses itself physically in a passionate act, to which God has attached a very great bodily pleasure. Through the use of that act, children are eventually born into the world. It is an innate instinct, which forms the physical basis of what we call sex attraction. The pleasure connected with it either directly or indirectly, may be rightfully enjoyed only by those who have entered into the married state. In other words, in return for the sacrifices which a true husband and wife are bound to make in the course of their wedded lives, Almighty God gives them the strict right to certain bodily pleasures.

Looked upon in this light, sex is something very beautiful, something very sacred, and something very reasonable. Because it is something sacred, we should discuss it reverently, as we would any other sacred subject. And yet how confused are our ideas with regard to it! Many good people actually quake when it is brought up for intelligent discussion. What is the reason for this narrow outlook concerning sex?

In many Catholic homes, the subject of sex is never discussed because the parents do not know how to explain it properly or in becoming words. As a result, young people get the idea that sex is something terrible. Add to this the cheap, tawdry ideas that are spread by newspapers, magazines, motion pictures, and novels — the dirty jokes that deal with abnormalities of sex — and the distorted view that the world gives us, as though everything we did were motivated by sexual desires. Many derive their first ideas on this important and delicate subject from the worst possible sources. It might have been from the conversation of the older fellows at the corner "hangout" or from some of the girls who "knew all the answers"; it might have been from some "wise" boy or girl companion or from a filthy booklet that fell into their hands — whatever the origin of their knowledge, you may be sure that they got a rather poor idea of it all.

It's the job of a father for his son and a mother for her daughter to give information about sex. Mine is to give you a reasonable explanation of the instincts that arise in every one of us, at one time or another. It is not wrong to have these instincts, but it is wrong to *deliberately* take the pleasure that may spring from them, unless you have received that right from Almighty God, in the sacrament of Matrimony. The instincts toward sex pleasure were not given you for their own sake, but to lead you on to the tremendous dignity of motherhood and fatherhood. Therefore, any deliberate enjoyment of those pleasures, by those who are not married, is a serious sin against the virtue of purity.

Besides the pleasure which is reserved only to married people, there is another kind, called social pleasure, which springs from association with our fellow human beings. You spend many happy hours in the company of other people. There may be certain priests or nuns whom you like to visit. And, of course, every normal young man (or young woman) enjoys the companionship of any attractive member of the opposite sex. That is the way the Lord has made us;

if we didn't enjoy the company of others, society would fall apart, because we'd all want to be hermits.

The big problem that we shall have to face all our life is seeing to it that our social pleasures, which are certainly not sinful, do not lead us into sexual pleasures. Why? Because any deliberate enjoyment of sexual pleasures, except by those who are lawfully married to each other, is always a serious sin.

For the sake of clarity, in view of the fact that purity is such an all important yet difficult virtue, let me briefly point out the principal offenses against it.

Generally speaking, we can sin against the virtue of purity in two ways — by thought and by action. There is a very important distinction to bear in mind about bad thoughts. You'll spare yourself a great deal of anxiety if you succeed in grasping this distinction clearly. It is *not* a sin *to have* bad thoughts. We're all bothered with bad thoughts, from time to time; we'll be bothered with them as long as we live. But, it *is* a sin *to deliberately and freely take pleasure* in a bad thought. For example, I may have a bad thought for a minute or so, before I realize what I am doing. If, as soon as I realize that is a bad thought, I deliberately refuse to take any pleasure in it, then I certainly have committed no sin. As a matter of fact, I've performed an act of virtue, by refusing to consent to that unlawful pleasure.

But what if I try to get rid of a bad thought, and I can't? As long as you don't want that bad thought, and you have made an honest effort to turn your mind to something else, there's no sin at all. In other words, without free and deliberate consent, you can never sin seriously. The best thing to do, when you realize that you have a bad thought, is to say a little prayer, like "Jesus, help me!" Then, turn your attention to something else, like your homework, or the radio, or what you're going to do that evening or the next day. If you do that, you never need fear that the Lord will hold you responsible for bad thoughts.

With regard to bad actions, we can sin by the misuse of our eyes, our ears, our tongues, and our sense of touch. We sin with our eyes when we look at dirty books or magazines, or when we read immoral books, or attend rotten shows. By dirty pictures, I mean suggestive drawings and pictures. By immoral books and magazines, I mean ones that deliberately and consistently play up violation of the sixth and ninth commandments. As for dirty shows, first of all there are the burlesque shows. There may have been a time when they were all right, but they're certainly wrong now. In addition, there are certain night clubs, whose floor shows are most objectionable. As for stage shows and movies, follow the Legion of Decency. To deliberately go to a "C" class show, without any justifying reason, is a sin.

We sin through the use of our ears and tongue by freely listening to and telling dirty stories, and by using foul and suggestive language. But our discussion of these particular faults will come later, when we consider them as a violation of the virtue of charity.

We sin through our sense of touch, either by touching ourselves, or by touching others, in an impure manner. As far as touching ourselves is concerned, of course there is no question of sin, when it comes to washing our bodies, or changing our clothes, or doing anything of a similar nature. Always remember that God is most reasonable in His laws; He doesn't expect the impossible. As a matter of medical fact, one of the best natural aids to purity is to keep your body clean at all times.

With regard to touching others in an impure manner, I believe you know what is wrong and what is right. The general principle is this: It is wrong for you to *deliberately* arouse your own passions (that is, to experience sexual pleasure) or to *deliberately* arouse the passions of the person with whom you happen to be. You have no right to the enjoyment of those pleasures, until you have accepted the responsibilities and the sacrifices that God meant to go with them.

What about kissing your girl friend or your boy friend? Never forget that a kiss is supposed to be a symbol of something sacred. It is meant to be a pledge of your mutual love and respect. It is not meant to be something that is handed out indiscriminately, like a street car transfer. I wouldn't give you an old "yo-yo" top for the "blarney-stone" type of girl, the kind that has been kissed by everyone but the Good Humor

Man. That is why the Catholic Church frowns upon any kind of a kissing game (like Post Office, Spin the Bottle, Flashlight, Blackout, or any other of the euphonious but perfectly obvious osculatory exhibitions); not because they are necessarily sinful, but because they are always dangerous, and certainly cheapening to the true idea of love.

Hand in hand with the practice of the virtue of purity goes the problem of drink, because drink has a tendency to weaken our self-control. It is difficult enough to keep clean and pure under ordinary circumstances, but when you start drinking it is twice as hard.

As a general rule, young people drink to be smart, and not because they like it or because they need it. They think that it makes them quite a "character" if they get "feeling good" at a party or after a dance. Of course, the fact that they may be griping a lot of other people in the crowd (and perhaps their own partners) never occurs to them. They think they had a great time at the party; but the truth is, they might just as well have stayed at home. After a few drinks, they didn't know where they were, anyway.

What is the Catholic Church's teaching about drink? If you can use drink correctly — that is, temperately — there is absolutely no question of sin. However, the Church points out the danger involved in drinking, especially for younger people. She insists that you watch your step. If you cannot drink without going to excess, "smarten up" and keep away from it entirely. There is a real danger, if you start drinking young, that you may fall a victim to drunkenness when you are older.

Young ladies, especially, take my advice. Don't go around with young men who are heavy drinkers. Not only is it a fact that they can't regard you very highly, when they would escort you in that condition, but there is always the danger that you might fall in love with a drinker and marry him. If you do, God help you! Your life on this earth will be just one cross after another. Any experienced priest will confirm my warning upon this point. There is only one thing worse than being a drunkard and that's being married to one.

One final point, in connection with the virtue of purity. Not only is it a sin to deliberately consent to any pleasures springing from the sexual instincts (unless, of course, you have received that right from God in the sacrament of Matrimony) but it is also a sin to freely and deliberately place yourself in an occasion where you *probably* will consent to such pleasures (unless you have a *serious* reason for doing so). To put it into plain language, if you commit sin every time, or practically every time, you go for a ride or park, you are bound to quit taking those rides and parking. If you commit sin practically every time you go out with a certain person, you either have to quit sinning, or quit going with that person. If you are guilty of the sin of impurity, practically every time you go to a certain club, or show, or house, then you must stay away from those places.

By this time, a good number of you may be thinking to yourselves, "Gosh, does the Catholic Church expect us to go through life wrapped in cellophane? Being a good Catholic seems to mean that you can't have any fun at all!"

That's wrong! It is not merely the Catholic Church's law, it is God's law! The Church does want you to have a "good time." The more enjoyment and the bigger "kick" you get out of life, the better she likes it. Because she places certain restrictions around the use of sexual pleasure, she is not trying to cramp your style or spoil your life. Those restrictions are emphasized by her to insure your happiness and to safeguard it, just as the ropes around certain parts of a beach are put there, not to lessen your enjoyment of the sport of swimming, but to minimize any possibility of drowning. Beyond those ropes, you might get caught in the undertow and lose your life. It is the same with the restrictions around sexual pleasure. If they were not there, you might get caught in the undertow of passion, and wreck your soul.

Why are danger signs put up on certain sections of skating ponds? To cut down or to do away with your enjoyment of ice skating? No, they're put there, because of the possibility that you might otherwise break through the thin ice and lose your life. Again, that is the Church's attitude in regard to the danger signs she places around sex. She is more concerned with your permanent happiness than she is with any passing thrill. Please believe that the Church lays down no unreasonable restrictions on sex pleasure. Some day, when you are a great deal older and have a family of your own, you'll realize this, too, and be thankful to her.

Purity is a virtue that challenges our strength and our courage. Anyone can be impure, but only those who are strong (with the help of God's grace, which He will never deny you) can be consistently pure. That is why the poet said, "My strength is as the strength of ten, because my heart is pure." The Catholic Church's teaching on purity requires genuine sacrifice and constant struggle against our lower impulses. But, don't forget, you're not walking the road toward heaven alone. You have Christ to help you fight your battles. Receive Him into your heart frequently in Holy Communion. Pray to our Blessed Lady and to Saint Joseph. Ask them to obtain for you the grace and the strength, the courage and the generosity, to model your life after theirs. And, above all, always keep before your mind the magnificent reward that our Lord has promised to those who are pure: "Blessed are the pure of heart, for they shall see God."

Chapter 4

THE "CHIN GANG"

THE story is told of a wise old pastor who asked his congregation to read over the twenty-ninth chapter of the gospel according to St. Matthew, in preparation for his sermon on the following Sunday. The next Sunday, when it came time to preach, he asked all those who had read the prescribed chapter to raise their hand. More than half the people in the church did so. Then the pastor smiled at them, very indulgently, and said, "That's why the subject of my sermon this morning will be 'Telling Lies.' There is no twenty-ninth chapter in St. Matthew's gospel."

Whether or not this story applies, all of us can profit by a little thought, not only on lying, but on all the sins of the tongue. Why? Because, next to the practice of the virtue of purity, the most common obstacle we encounter on the road to heaven is the misuse of our tongue. That is why St. James said, "If any man offend not in speech, the same is a perfect man."

The general principle to guide us, in determining what is sinful speech and what is not, is this: Almighty God gave us the faculty of speech so that we might praise Him, that we might live in peace and charity with our neighbors and speak the truth. Any use of our speech contrary to this general principle is sinful, either mortal (serious) or venial (slight), depending to a great extent upon the circumstances.

One of the most common misuses of the faculty of speech is lying. To lie is to tell a falsehood with the intention of deceiving. As a general rule, lying is a venial sin, although it can become a mortal sin, if serious consequences are involved. There is no such thing, therefore, as a "white lie." All lies are black, inasmuch as they are the misuse of a faculty given us by God. However (and this will be a source of consolation and relief for you), there are certain expressions, in popular usage, which might seem like lies; but if we analyze them further, we will see that they are not.

For example, let us imagine that you have been invited to see the "brand-new" baby of some married friends of yours. You are ushered into the room in which is the center of attraction. As you gaze down at the red faced infant in the cradle, you might be tempted to repeat the obvious truth that most babies, at that age, are far from ravishing beauties. But the situation calls for common sense and tact. Custom demands that you turn to the proud mother and the strutting father and make some time-honored, inane remark, like: "My, what a perfectly adorable youngster. He has your nose, but he has Harry's eyes!"

Would that be a lie? Of course not. Imagine what

would happen if you turned to the beaming young parents, and said, "Cheer up. None of them look very human for the first couple of months." Even if you escaped with only minor bodily injuries, you may be sure that you would never be invited to that home again.

Just one more example of what is certainly not lying. You meet an old schoolmate on the occasion of some social affair. You haven't seen her for years, and, as far as you're concerned, if you never see her again, it will be too soon. However, common decency demands that you drag out some kind of conversation, however dull it may be. Finally, you see the opportunity to bring the verbal encounter to what you hope will seem like a graceful conclusion. Quick as a dive-bomber, you pounce upon the opportunity and, as you gracefully glide away, you say very gaily, like a radio announcer trying to slip in a commercial: "Now, don't forget. If you're ever up around our side of town, you must drop in on us and have dinner."

You don't mean it, and she knows that you don't mean it. If she ever dropped in on you, you'd drop, too.

Both of these examples, and many others that are very familiar, are instances of what might be called the use of "social oil." They are not lies, because there is no intention to deceive. Rather, they are the oil that makes the wheels of everyday life run smoothly.

Think what a terrible life this would be if we

couldn't use the familiar phrases that really mean nothing. Even the most thick-skinned among us would soon give up in despair, if people did not have some perfectly harmless means of sparing our feelings.

The second way we sin by our tongues is by using God's name, or the names of the saints, without the reverence that is due to them. Contrary to the belief of some people, however, the misuse of God's name is not a mortal, but a venial sin. I do not wish to detract from the reverence due to God's holy name, but you should know this, because some individuals who are guilty of this practice refrain from receiving Holy Communion, feeling that they are in the state of mortal sin. On the contrary, were they to receive Communion more frequently, they would find it a splendid means of breaking themselves of this shameful habit.

Using God's name as an expression of anger, surprise, or to emphasize a point, reminds me of the alibi that you hear most frequently, in defense or explanation of it. People will say, "I really don't mean to be irreverent. It's just a habit with me." And, of course, you're supposed to say, "Oh well, as long as it's a habit, go right ahead."

On the contrary, any habit can be broken, if you're man or woman enough to make the necessary effort. If, for example, every time you found yourself using God's name irreverently, you got up fifteen minutes earlier the next morning, or put a quarter in the poor box at church, you would very soon break the habit.

The trouble with too many of us is that we seem to have adopted the wrong theme song as regards bad habits. It's a song that was quite popular a few years ago. The name of it is "Wishing," and the main line is "Wishing will make it so." We wish we didn't do this, and we wish we didn't do that. We wish we could be more charitable in our speech, we wish we went to Holy Communion oftener, and so on and on. The trouble with too many of us is that we have "wish-bones" instead of backbones.

The third way we sin by the misuse of our tongue springs from our failure to watch over our speech at home. But that is such an important matter, that the whole next chapter will be devoted to it.

Now we come face to face with that great problem in social life — dirty stories. Much to my sorrow, honesty and truth demand that both men and women need to be warned against telling dirty stories.

The saddest feature about this type of really doubtful entertainment is the fact that dirty story tellers not only sin themselves, but they are very often also the occasion of sin for their listeners. These risqué artists think that they are the life of the party. As a matter of fact, though, they are really the death of the party, as far as their friends' souls are concerned. They think they are being very funny, but their sense of humor is certainly distorted. It doesn't take much wit to see the point of a dirty joke or story.

To be fair about this whole matter, though, we must make a distinction between dirty stories and vulgar stories. Vulgar stories, as a general rule, are not sinful — unless, of course, there is a question of scandal — but dirty stories are. Some of the funniest stories ever told have been vulgar ones. Usually, it is not too difficult to distinguish between vulgar stories and dirty stories. The late "Chick" Sales is an example of a man who told vulgar stories, the kind that we refer to as "outhouse" stories, or that describe some of the natural functions of the body. Their purpose is not to arouse our passions. On the other hand, dirty stories are those whose subject matter, of their very nature, tends to stir up our lower nature. Occasionally, it may happen that a story or a remark is on the border line. But, more times than not, we know very well what kind of a story we are telling or listening to.

You wouldn't take poisoned food into your body, or give it to your guests. Well, a dirty story is far harder on your soul than poisoned food is on your body. It's hard enough as it is to stay clean and pure, without going out of your way to look for trouble. When you listen to one of those stories, you're "leading with your chin." Never forget that the very tongue that you use to peddle filth will be offered to our Blessed Lord as a resting place, when you receive Him in Holy Communion. Don't make a Judas' kiss out of your Communions!

Almighty God realizes what a difficult proposition

you are up against. It's almost impossible nowadays to go any place, or work any place, without hearing the dirty stories and off-color remarks that are being passed around. What can you do about them? What does the Lord expect you to do about them?

If you are the one who is telling these stories the answer is very simple: Cut them out! If it is the crowd that you go around with, and you have to go with them, try not to laugh at the jokes, or to encourage them. If it happens at the place where you work, try to pay as little attention as possible to them. One thing, however, I advise you not to do. Don't start preaching to others. It won't get you any place, and all that you'll succeed in doing is to stir up for yourself a lot of hatred and petty persecution. Your fellow workers will go out of their way to tell these stories in your presence, or make remarks simply to get a "rise" out of you.

The best principle to adopt is this: If you can avoid these dirty stories and remarks, do so. If you can't, don't worry. Do your best not to think about the stories, and frequently repeat little prayers, like "Jesus, help me!" Then leave the rest up to our Lord. He knows the "spot" you are in, and He is most reasonable.

Perhaps the most universal of human faults is gossiping. No consideration of sins of the tongue would be complete without a reference to gossip — that is, talking about the faults (real, or imagined) and the doings of our neighbors. From time immemorial gossip has been regarded as a woman's sin, but I think that accusation is unfair to women. From my own experience, I would say that men gossip just as much as women, though they may not be quite as expert at it.

Of course, we all know that it is wrong to say untrue things about our neighbors, but what so many of us forget is that it is wrong to tell even the truth about our neighbor, when it will seriously hurt his reputation. The only exception occurs when our neighbor has publicly forfeited his or her reputation. Therefore, the old alibi, "but every word I said about her was the gospel truth," doesn't excuse us in the least.

Gossip is a cowardly thing. Very often we wouldn't dare repeat it in the presence of the accused. We have to whisper it behind his or her back, when our neighbor hasn't the ghost of a chance for self-defense.

Gossip is a very ignorant thing. It doesn't require much brain power to figure out that your neighbor has faults. We all have faults. I wouldn't want my faults broadcast all over a neighborhood. Why shouldn't I feel the same way toward you?

Gossip is a cheap thing. We gain the momentary attention of other people at the terrible price of some one else's reputation. Make no mistake about it — a real gossiper is despised by honorable people.

Gossiping reflects an inferiority complex. We think that by tearing other people down we are building ourselves up, but we're not. We're merely exposing our own weaknesses.

Without any exaggeration, some people are human "vacuum cleaners," always on the search for a "little dirt." If they spent half the time working on their own faults, that they waste in ruining their neighbors' reputation, they would be domestic saints.

In connection with these members of the "chin gang," an incident from the life of our Blessed Lord will provide plenty of food for meditation. It is the incident of the woman who was found guilty of the sin of adultery.

The punishment for that sin, among the Jews, was death. A number of the Jews who hated our Blessed Lord and His teachings saw the opportunity to place Him in a very difficult position. They knew that He was continually preaching mercy toward sinners, and that, at the same time, He upheld the authority of the state. And so they decided to bring this poor unfortunate woman before our Lord, figuring that they had Him in a spot. If He was merciful and let her go, they would accuse Him of violating the laws of the state. But if He upheld the law of the state and said that she was deserving of death, they would say that He preached mercy toward sinners but did not practice it.

Of course our Lord was far too clever for them. He knew what a group of hypocrites they really were. And so He merely said, "Let him who is without sin among you cast the first stone." Then, stooping over,

He slowly began to trace in the sands at His feet the secret sins of those who were accusing the woman. One by one, as they saw their sins revealed, they slunk away, until finally no one was left but Christ and the sinful woman. Not a single one, mind you, of all who had been accusing her. Turning to the poor woman at His feet, our Blessed Lord said, "Woman, if no one else accuses you, neither do I. Go in peace, and sin no more."

Some day that very same Christ is going to be your judge and mine. Will He be merciful toward us, because we were always merciful toward others? Or will He be forced to trace our sins of gossip on the book of life, never to be erased by the fires of hell?

It depends upon us!

Chapter 5

STRICTLY "OFF THE RECORD"

"CHARITY begins at home!" We've heard that statement time and again, but has it ever made any deep or lasting impression on us, or is it only another remark that we throw off in conversation? One of the things that it should mean is that, in obeying the great commandment of our Lord to love our neighbors, we begin by loving those who are the closest to us — our own family. It is a peculiar thing, but we generally show the worst side of our nature to those whom we should love the most. The reason may be that they are the only ones who, after knowing them, will continue to put up with our failings and faults.

For example, somebody's dad may be a grand person down at work, a regular fellow with all the men, and a perfect gentleman in his dealings with the women employees. When it comes to money, he's the soul of generosity, a free spender. Whenever he's out with the "boys," he always reaches for the check, and most of the time he manages to get it.

But when that man comes home from work, what a difference! You'd swear he was a Dr. Jekyll and

Mr. Hyde, a regular dual personality. The minute he comes through the door at home, he expects everyone to drop what they're doing and begin to wait on him. You'd think that he was the only one in the house who ever did an honest day's work. Regardless of the circumstances, if the meal isn't served right on the "dot," or if it doesn't suit his taste perfectly, he becomes positively indignant. He expects a "Pump Room" menu on a "White Castle" budget. After a meal is over, he seldom (if ever!) compliments mother on it, but stalks majestically into the parlor, picks up his paper, lights his pipe or cigar, relaxes in his armchair, and — God help the poor soul who dares to disturb his regal repose.

Mother may have worked twice as hard as dad all day, but he never stops to realize that she might appreciate a change of scenery. If she has the unmitigated nerve to suggest that they go out somewhere together, he's almost certain to start growling about how hard a day he had. Yet he is the very same person who would go blocks out of his way to help a pretty stranger, or who would not dream of asking a young lady employee to work overtime.

And when it comes to money, his theme song to mother is always the same sorrowful refrain: "Do you think that money grows on trees?" Money may go through his own hands like water, but he expects it to go through her hands like molasses. He constantly preaches about her extravagance, and her foolish spending, and then, in one afternoon at the races, or in one evening at his card club or a tavern, he spends enough to balance her budget for a week. During his courtship days, the best was none too good for her. Now, when he pays the bill for her new hat, you'd think that he was going to need a blood transfusion.

But, is dad the only member of the family who is lacking in charity? Let's take a look at mother.

All the priests in the parish think that mother is just the last word. She always has such a beautiful smile for the "Fathers," and she is never too busy to help out with any parish activity. "Oh, Father, I'm only too happy to give you a hand!" The women in the parish altar society, and in her bridge club, think that she is marvelous, too. "I don't know how she does it, with the large family that she has." Mother always manages to appear so perfectly poised. In a mixed gathering she just oozes personality. She is the despair of all her married women acquaintances, and the envy of all their husbands. And when the children's friends meet her, they can't get over her kindness — she's just too, too divine!

But at home, when just the family is present — ah, that's another story! Then she "crabs" about every little thing that goes wrong, complains that she is working herself into an early grave, that she never has a decent thing to wear. The children get on her nerves, and she always "harps" on how much she has done for them, how she has worked her fingers to the bone for them, and how ungrateful they are in return. And as for father, she married him for better or for worse, and to hear her tell it, she's been getting the worst of it, ever since. To think of the wonderful men that she might have got! And so it goes on, far into the night.

Next, from behind the scenes, in this review of family life, comes the son. At school, his professors point to him with pride, and his companions classify him a "prince of a fellow." In the crowd he mixes with, the girls think him quite a "catch," he's so thoughtful and such a gentleman. His own girl friend thinks the sun rises and sets on him. Why, he can't do enough for her! Why should he walk her home, a few blocks from the theater, and tire her out? (You know how hard it is to walk any distance, in high heeled pumps.) No, he insists on calling a cab to take her home, or he manages to sneak off with the family car. When it comes to a question of doing any work for her, he'd gladly dig ditches with his fingernails, if she'd only smile at him.

But when you see young Lochinvar at home, with only his immediate family for an audience, as the old song used to go, "You'd be surprised!" If mother dares to ask him to soil his hands, by taking out the ashes or by cutting the grass, you'd think, from the way he moans, that she was asking him to dig the Panama Canal with his bare hands. He never does anything promptly. He has to be pleaded with before he goes into motion of any kind. The only reason he does anything at all, in the long run, is the fear of being reported to father, or of having his allowance stopped. He's always quarreling with his brothers about something or other, and he is the bane of his sister's existence. To hear him complain, you'd think his life was just one long round of persecution. He never goes out of his way to be nice to mother or father, or to help them in any way — in fact, he spends most of his time at home figuring how to get out of the house before they pin any work on him. And from the way he looks at his sister's boy friends, you'd think she was being courted by Dracula or Frankenstein.

Last, but certainly far from least (in her own estimation), comes daughter. The nuns at school, who teach her, think she is a very lovely pupil, always willing to lend them a hand in any work they might have to do. Her girl friends like her, too, because she doesn't mind sharing her homework with them, or even helping them get a date. And, to the boys, she's just a dream come true! When she talks to them in person, or coos to them over the telephone, her every word is like a caress. Butter would melt in her mouth. And her clothes — why she always looks so chic at a party you'd think that she was a cover girl, or a manikin at one of the swanky stores. You'd wonder if she were being paid by Schiaparelli or Daché, as she floats around in a heavenly aroma that faintly suggests Chanel No. 5.

But again, look at the other side of the picture. In

the intimacy of her own home, you would never recognize daughter as the same glamorous creature. She is like another Cinderella, after the stroke of midnight. She is never neatly dressed, except when she is going out on a date, and you'd think that "curlers" grew in her hair, she wears them around the house so often. Speaking of a lovely disposition, there was never a prima donna more temperamental than she. She can cry at the drop of a hat. When it comes to housework, you'd think it was a sacrilege to ask her to soil her dainty white fingers and her gleaming red fingernails. To hear her complain, you'd think that she was an inmate of a concentration camp. Her constant topic of conversation, in a voice that is anything but musical, is the clothes she needs, that her girl friends have, but her parents won't buy for her. As far as she is concerned, it's going to be her parents' fault if she never gets a husband — it will serve them right for the shabby way they always dressed her, and the miserable allowance they begrudged her, and the liberty they failed to grant.

This picture has been greatly overdrawn, but only to emphasize the essential points more clearly. If you're honest with yourself, you'll have to admit that here and there, some of the words apply to you or your parents. Yet that picture should not be true in any respect, because underneath the superficial faults of the individual members of any good ordinary Catholic family, there is a deep, mutual love. That love comes to the surface on the occasion of sickness or death in the family. You realize it keenly, when you are away from home and experience the pangs of homesickness for the first time.

But why should our love be submerged, like a submarine, only to come up at a time of trouble? Why should we wait for a domestic crisis? Why can't we make our home a permanent center of real love? The world can be, and very often is, extremely harsh and cruel. There should be some place to find genuine love, and sympathy, and understanding. If we're going to be rude, or angry, or mean, let's be that way toward strangers, toward people with whom we have only a nodding acquaintance. Usually, we don't mean the harsh things we say at home in a moment of anger or vexation. Yet those words often cut deeply. When we kneel at the casket of one of our family, our bitterest regrets will spring from the memory of the little acts of unkindness we directed toward them in their lifetime. Don't wait until your mother or father, or your brothers and sisters, are dead, to show them your love. Show it now!

One objection is probably lurking in the back of your mind. "It's easy enough for Father to tell us to be charitable toward the other members of our family, but he never lived in a family like mine."

Some of you, perhaps, are thinking of parents who consistently fail to show you the slightest consideration, and who continually ignore your smallest demands. Some of you are thinking of brothers and sisters who are forever nagging and picking at you. You young men are thinking of fathers and mothers who never seem to realize that you've grown up, and of sisters who are always "getting into your hair." And some of you young ladies are wondering if I could possibly imagine just how unspeakably old fashioned your folks are, and how difficult they make it for you to live a successful social life. "Can you imagine having to be home by midnight!"

Never forget that you have faults and peculiarities, just as much as the rest of the family. Only God is perfect! You've certainly got to be willing to overlook their faults, if you expect them to overlook yours. And be prepared to go three-fourths of the way. No one ever solved family problems by only going halfway.

Ask our Blessed Lady today, and throughout all the remaining days of your life, to help make your home what her divine Son meant it to be, when He raised marriage to the dignity of a sacrament — "a little bit of heaven" on earth. Ask her who was the Queen of the most perfect of all families, the Holy Family at Nazareth, to help you do your part toward accomplishing this by never letting you forget the meaning of the expression: "Charity begins at home."

Chapter 6

THE GIFT OF GIFTS

WHENEVER a non-Catholic asks for instructions, I always ask him what it was that led him to the Catholic Church. My motive for asking that question is not mere curiosity, although curiosity does enter into it. It is rather to build up a convert psychology. Perhaps what led that person to the true faith may be the means, with God's help, of leading others to it. In any event, such questioning always helps me broaden my own spiritual outlook on the non-Catholic viewpoint. It has been my good fortune to hear many different reasons for conversion, but here is one that I shall never forget. I heard it a few years ago, as a curate, "back of the yards," in Chicago.

One evening a young man, about twenty-four years of age, walked into the rectory and said that he would like to take instructions in the Catholic religion. After a few minutes spent in trying to put him at ease, I fired my customary question at him.

"Why have you decided to become a Catholic?"

His answer was startling, to say the least. "I'll tell you, Father. I go around with a couple of Catholic lads, and we generally do quite a bit of drinking on Saturday night. In the two years that I've been going out with them, no matter how drunk they got on Saturday night, they never missed Mass on Sunday morning. So I decided that any religion that could exercise such a powerful influence over anyone deserved a little investigation on my part."

When the young man finished his story, I could only marvel at the strange ways of the Lord. But I wondered what sort of idea his Catholic friends had of the Mass, when they would go to it in such a condition. In fact, I often wonder how many people have grasped the true idea of the Mass. Traveling around as a missionary, and standing in the rear of the Church, at the various Masses, the things you see are sometimes simply amazing.

For example, there are the "pew hogs." They get the end of the pew and hold it, like the Maginot Line. You've practically got to be a pole vaulter to get by them successfully. You lunge over them when you enter Church; you squeeze by them to go up to Communion, and when you return; and, of course, they stay a few minutes after Mass, which necessitates a final leap on your part, to get into the aisle. The attitude of these people seems to be: "I got here first, so I deserve the best part of the pew. If you don't like it, get here ahead of time."

Then there are those devout souls who seem to have effected a compromise between kneeling, sitting, and standing — what we might call a "three point landing." Regardless of their posture, however, they never appear to be perfectly comfortable.

Next are the members of the PBI — the prayer book investigators. They're always thumbing through a prayer book (preferably someone else's) and glancing at the various holy pictures, memento cards, and personal souvenirs entombed in its pages.

As you gaze with wondering eye, from the rear of the church, you may see every type of activity, from downright repose to angelic attention. Some people twist and squirm in the pew to such an extent, that you're almost tempted to believe they are afflicted with St. Vitus' dance. Others appear to be perfectly bored, not just at the interval when the announcements are being read or the sermon is being preached — occasionally, at that time, there is reasonable justification for such a reaction — but during the celebration of the Mass itself!

When Mass is over, the way some people struggle to get out, you'd think the church was on fire. For them, Thanksgiving only means the last Thursday in November. However, these "devout" souls are not nearly as reprehensible as the "big-time" operators, whose every moment is precious. They can't even wait for the Mass to be over, before they dash out of the church. When the priest turns around to give the last blessing, they seem to think he is saying, "ready — set — go!"

But these are not the first to "escape" from the church. That intrepid vanguard of the last ones in and the first ones out always bravely leads the way. They're the "sharpshooters" in the rear of the church, the "one-knee brigade," who bolster up the rear wall at the late Masses.

As a fit running-mate for the "sharpshooters," there is that squad of all-Americans who seem to have taken a solemn vow never to get to Mass on time. Week in, and week out, spring, summer, winter, or fall, the same crowd comes trooping in late. Of course, they take care that they are never seriously late. They know very well that it is not a mortal sin, unless the veil has already been taken from the chalice. But what they seem to forget is that to *deliberately* miss even the smallest part of Mass is something wrong.

Far worse than any of these, are people who miss Sunday Mass frequently and deliberately. It has been said, perhaps with some degree of truth, that there is a special punishment in hell for such. Our Blessed Lord dealt very mercifully with sins resulting from human weakness and from passion. But those who miss Mass deliberately fall into a different category of sinners. They simply refuse to obey God. And we know how God punished the fallen angels for one sin of disobedience.

"Ah, but no one would deliberately miss Mass on Sunday." No? Just take a look around your church on Christmas Day or Easter. Where does that great crowd come from? Too many of them are "Easter birds" coming home to roost.

Last in the scale of Mass offenders are those who are critical of the time consumed by Mass. They speak in a very praiseworthy fashion about the priest who says a "fast Mass," and complain most bitterly about the priest who is a "slow poke." How hateful it is to hear this jeremiad, when non-Catholics are present! Why begrudge the Lord a few extra minutes of our time? Have you known people, too, who would travel for miles just to find a church where Mass is celebrated more quickly? They can afford to stay out till three o'clock in the morning, celebrating, but they can't seem to stand five or ten minutes extra with the Lord. Now, we're not expected to like to attend a Mass where the priest is extraordinarily slow. But you can't expect every priest to be a "streak of lightning." Some priests are naturally much slower than others. When a priest says Mass he is not trying for a speed record. He is offering a gift to God!

What is the cause of these various attitudes toward the Mass? Honestly, I believe they can all be traced back to one source, to more or less ignorance of the real nature of the Mass. It would do us all good to brush up on that, not that we're guilty of any of the spiritual breaches mentioned, but to prevent our falling into such habits later on in life.

First of all, the Mass is a gift. From time immemorial, men and women have given gifts to those they love. Almighty God Himself demanded that the chosen people in the Old Testament offer gifts to Him as a sign of their love. In fact, He stated very explicitly what was to be given to Him. With the coming of Christ in the New Testament, all these old gifts were to be done away with. They were no longer pleasing to God. Since the death of Christ, only one gift is acceptable to Him. That is the gift of His own Son, which takes place in the Mass.

The Mass is no ordinary gift; it is the *greatest of all gifts*. We measure the value of a gift, not by its price tag, but by the sacrifice it cost the giver. The greater the sacrifice, the greater the gift. When a man lays down his life for his country, he is said to have made the supreme sacrifice, because he has surrendered his greatest earthly possession — his life. When our Blessed Lord laid down His life for us on Calvary, He made the supreme sacrifice of all times, because He gave up the greatest of all lives. Since the Mass is the unbloody representation or re-enactment of Christ's death on the cross, it is logically the greatest of all gifts.

Best of all, the Mass is a *gift that I offer to God* in union with the priest. The emphasis there is most decidedly on the words, *I offer*. Being present at Mass, therefore, is not like witnessing a movie, or a football game, or a parade, where I am present only as a spectator. I attend Mass as a participator in the action of the Mass; I am a co-offerer of the sacrifice. That is why the priest, after he has placed the wine in the chalice preparatory to the sacrifice, turns to the people and begins the prayer, "Pray brethren, that *your* sacrifice and mine may be acceptable to Almighty God."

In the last analysis, it is not the priest who offers up the Mass; it is really our Blessed Lord Himself. He uses the priest as an instrument, just as I might use a pen to write a letter, the only difference, of course, being that the priest has free will.

The great gift of the Mass is offered up to God, for four distinct reasons or purposes. These purposes are accomplished, whether I am aware of it or not.

First, every Mass is an expression of my complete and absolute dependence upon Almighty God. He is my creator, and I am His creature. Reason demands that I acknowledge this fact. This I do, every time I am present at Mass.

Second, every Mass is a supreme act of thanksgiving upon my part. All that I am, or have, or hope to be, I owe to God, my redeemer, and my judge. What more perfect way could I find to thank Him than through His own divine Son?

Third, every Mass constitutes a perfect means of asking God for everything I need. Who among us does not stand very badly in need of many, many things, not only in the natural order — such as good health, a good job, peace in the family, etc., but especially in the supernatural order — stronger faith, a deeper hope, and a more active charity?

Finally, the Mass affords every one of us the divinely appointed means of begging God's pardon for the many offenses we have committed against Him. What a source of consolation it should be to realize that we can join with Christ Himself in offering atonement for our sins.

When you realize how much the Mass accomplishes for you, you will want to examine your attitude toward it. While you've been very faithful about going to Mass on Sunday, have you been getting anything out of it? Have you been going to Mass merely because your parents make you go, or because your girl friend insists on it, or because everyone in your crowd goes? Do you go because it is a habit you acquired as a youngster, or because you wouldn't "feel right" if you didn't go, or because you're afraid to stay away? Has Sunday Mass been dull and monotonous, something that you have to endure every week? If it has, it's time to change your mind.

It is a real sacrifice to get out of bed on Sunday morning, especially when you've been out late the night before — that's just the point! Offer up that sacrifice to the Lord. Realize that you're going to Mass on Sunday morning, when you'd much rather stay in bed, at a sacrifice of your time and convenience, to express your dependence upon Almighty God, to thank Him for the helps He gave you during the past week, to beg His pardon for the mistakes you made, and to ask His assistance for the coming week.

The ideal way, of course, to attend Mass would be to say the same prayers as the priest. Those prayers can be found in the missal, or Mass book. You can purchase one of those Mass books, in English, at and religious goods store, for a very nominal sum of money. And if you use that Mass book four Sundays in a row, you won't have any difficulty after that in following the Mass. Try it and see. Maybe you prefer to say your rosary or to use a prayer book. You may like just to kneel there and recall our Lord's death on the cross. The main thing to keep in mind is the reason why you have come to church. Then, you're bound to profit by the Mass.

Ask our Blessed Lord to make the sacrifice of the Mass become exactly what He intended it should become in your life, the great central act of your religion.

Chapter 7

THE PERFECT REMEDY

EVER since we were children, we've been told how to go to Confession; and yet, many of us make such a difficult job of it, that we fail to get the results our Blessed Lord intended to come from it. A few months ago, in conversation with a prominent doctor at a dinner party, the subject of Confession happened to come up. The doctor gave me a perfect opening for a short exposition on the true idea of Confession, when he said, "Gosh, Father, I'd rather perform the most difficult operation than go to Confession." Naturally, I asked him why, and he replied that he was always "on edge" afterward, for fear that he might have forgotten something.

That doctor knew medicine from A to Z, but he certainly had the wrong idea of Confession. Our Lord never meant the confessional to be a torture chamber. He meant it to be a place where our souls would be refreshed. Confession was intended to be the original "pause that refreshes." With this thought in mind, let's briefly review our ideas on Confession, so that we may be certain to make good soul-satisfying ones from now on.

The first point to make clear is that there are two kinds of Confession, just as there are two kinds of baths. One kind of bath is the dip we take on a hot summer day, for example, to refresh ourselves. We plunge into the cooling waters, not because we are dirty, but because we want to regain our "pep." The other type of bath is the old-fashioned one that we used to take on Saturday night, the kind we took because we needed it.

We may go to Confession to refresh our soul spiritually, to stimulate our soul in the effort to serve God faithfully, to get the helps we need to keep from falling into sin. That's the reason, for example, why priests and sisters go to Confession frequently, even every week — not because they are constantly falling into serious sin, but to get God's help, through the medium of the sacrament, to continue on "the straight and narrow path." On the other hand, we may go to Confession, because we need it — because we are in the state of serious sin.

To put it briefly, you *may* go to Confession as often as you mention some slight sin, or some previously confessed serious or slight sin, for which you are again sorry. You *must* go to Confession, before receiving Holy Communion, as often as you are in the state of serious sin. Every adult Catholic who has reached the age of reason is also bound, by Church law, to go to Confession at least once a year.

Just in passing, recall the essential requirements for

a serious sin. Back in second grade, remember how glibly we would chant, "grievous matter, sufficient reflection, and full consent of the will"? That means: It must be something serious, I must know that it is serious, and I must do it freely. If one of those three conditions is lacking, there is no serious sin. Just as, for example, three things are necessary for a chocolate soda: chocolate flavoring, soda water, and ice cream. If one of those three is missing, you may have something else, but you haven't a chocolate soda.

The proper way of going to Confession consists of three stages: the time *before* you go to Confession (in other words, your preparation), the time *during* your Confession (that is, the actual telling of your sins), and the time *after* your Confession.

Before you can confess your sins, you must recall your offenses against God. Technically, this is known as the examination of conscience. It consists in looking back over your life, since the time of your last sincere Confession, and seeing in what way you may have broken God's laws or the laws of His Church. It is necessary, in the case of serious sins, that you state the kind of sin each one is, and the number of times you committed it. Some people get themselves all upset and worried for fear they might not be able to tell the exact number. I assure you, they are suffering from needless anxiety. Almighty God is most reasonable. He does not expect any of us to be human adding machines, or perfect bookkeepers. The way some people worry you'd think God was lying in wait and ready to pounce upon us, during Confession, for any little slips we might make.

There are two extremes to avoid in examining your conscience. One extremist is the sincere soul, who goes to Confession regularly, and yet spends a half hour or so examining his conscience. The other extremist is the person who rarely goes to the sacrament, and yet blithely plunges into the confessional without making any preparation whatsoever. The correct way, as always, is the happy medium. If you've been away from Confession for a long time, spend some time in getting ready. If you're still worried about your preparation, don't hesitate to ask the priest to help you — he will be only too glad to do so. If you go to Confession every month, or oftener, there is hardly reason for your taking more than a few minutes to examine your conscience.

Strange as it may sound, the most important part of your Confession is not the actual telling of your sins, but rather being sorry for them. A sin that you forget to tell in Confession can be and *is* forgiven because of the fact that, in a *sincere* Confession, you are sorry for all your sins, including the ones you have forgotten. But a sin is *never* forgiven, if you are not sorry for it.

Don't fall into the mistake of imagining that emotional sorrow is necessary for the forgiveness of sins. Very often it is not even possible to *feel* sorry. I mean that in Confession you don't have to work yourself into a state similar to the one you would experience if your mother or dad died. What is required is that you sincerely regret having offended the good Lord, and have an honest determination, with His help, not to sin again. If you say your act of contrition, and mean every word of it, you need never fear that your sorrow is not sufficient. The simplest, yet complete and perfect act of sorrow that I know is this:

"Oh my God, I'm sorry that I offended You, because I love You. With Your help, I'll try not to sin again."

If you are sorry for your sins *only* because of the *fear of hell*, you still have sufficient sorrow for the forgiveness of your sins, provided that that sorrow is joined to the use of the sacrament of Penance. This is known as imperfect contrition or attrition. Never forget this important fact with regard to Confession, for the day may come in your life when the *love of God* is not strong enough in your heart to make you regret having offended Him and you may need the *fear of hell* to rely upon for being sorry for your sins.

When you enter the confessional, begin your Confession by telling the priest the approximate time since your last Confession. Don't worry if you don't get the time exactly to the day, but try to come as close as you can. In that way, the priest gets a clearer idea of your spiritual background. If, for any reason, you were denied forgiveness in your previous Confession, don't fail to mention that fact.

In telling your actual sins, there are again two extremes to avoid. One extremist is the person who insists on telling the priest everything, except his latest operation. And, of course, the other extremist is a "mute, inglorious Milton," out of whom the priest has to dig nearly everything. The correct method is to tell your sins briefly, according to their kind and their number, if they are serious; if they are not serious, at least according to their kind.

When you have finished your statement, listen attentively to the advice the priest may think it necessary to give you. If he asks you any questions, answer them briefly and to the best of your ability. You wouldn't expect a doctor to be able to help you, if you didn't supply him with the information he considered necessary for your cure. Don't expect the priest, who has been appointed by God to be the physician of your soul, to read your mind.

You know, of course, that it is simply foolish to hold back a serious sin in Confession. Not only that Confession is worthless, but all your subsequent Confessions are of absolutely no value until that sin has been revealed. We are either sorry for all of our serious sins, or God does not forgive any of them. It would be perfectly ridiculous to imagine God acting otherwise. If you have ever made that mistake, just mention it in your next Confession, and the priest will straighten it out in no time at all.

Before absolving (that is, forgiving) you, the priest

will give you certain prayers to say as penance for your sins. If, for any reason, you do not understand the penance, ask the priest to kindly repeat it. If it consists of prayers that you don't know, tell the priest. Then, while the priest is saying the words of forgiveness in Latin, recite your act of contrition. Although it is not imperative, I would suggest that you say it loudly enough for the priest to hear it. If you get flustered and can't recall the act of contrition, simply tell God you're sorry, and that you'll try not to offend Him again.

When you leave the confessional, try to say your penance immediately, even though this is not absolutely necessary. It is better to say the prayers immediately to avoid the possibility of forgetting your penance. However, if for any reason you do happen to omit your penance, state that fact in your next Confession.

Now, what's hard about going to Confession, outside of the natural humiliation that is bound to come (which our Lord evidently intended) from confessing our weaknesses to another human being like ourselves?

Experience has taught some helpful things about Confession.

First, don't go to just any priest (unless, of course, circumstances happen to make it necessary), but shop around until you find a confessor who understands you. Then, go to him regularly. This may be rather difficult in small towns, but it is very simple in the larger ones. "But," you will say, "I thought all priests could forgive sins. Why go to one priest rather than another?" It is true that all authorized priests have the power to forgive sins; but so have all barbers and hairdressers the power to cut hair, they all get the hair off, but some of them do a much better job of it. You wouldn't go to just any barber or hairdresser, would you? You'd look around until you found one who did a very fine piece of work on you. It is the same with priests. Different priest confessors have different temperaments, just as penitents have different temperaments. Keep going to different priests, for Confession, until you get one who satisfies your temperament. By that I don't mean to keep searching until you get a confessor with a "deaf" ear. If you do, you'll be fooling yourself and never get anywhere in your spiritual life.

Secondly, don't be discouraged if you seem to be, or actually are, confessing the same sins every time. Maybe you could even have a record made of your confession, it changes so little from month to month. Is that a sign that your confessions are of no avail, that you're really not making sufficient effort to improve? No, it merely points out certain flaws in your character, that you will probably have to fight against all your life. Whatever happens, don't be like the little girl who hated to go to Confession, " 'Cause," she said sorrowfully, "I can never think of any new sins to tell." The Lord will always be satisfied with your old sins, provided you are truly sorry for them.

Lastly, don't expect to feel like a million dollars every time that you walk out of the confessional. You hear a lot of sermons about the peace, the joy, and the consolation of a good Confession, yet you may often feel exactly the same when you finish as you did before you started. You may sense no more spiritual elation after Confession than you would if you had just finished talking to the druggist or the butcher. The important thing is that you are certain your sins are forgiven. You have God's word for that! Your Confession does not depend, for its value and its efficacy, upon the arousing of your emotions. Our faith is not based upon anything so fickle, so changeable, or so tricky as our sentimental nature. On the contrary, it is rooted in the solid rock of reason. Thank God it is that way. Otherwise, we could seldom be certain that we had obtained God's forgiveness. What chance would most of us have to obtain God's pardon, if we had to display the sorrow of a Magdalen or a Peter?

The more you think about Confession and the great good it accomplishes, the more you marvel at God's wisdom and His generosity. What a horrible world this would be to live in, if we didn't have Confession to get us back on the right track when we slip!

Chapter 8

THE FOUNTAIN OF YOUTH

AT GRAMMAR school, my favorite subject was history. It was fascinating to read about what other people did in their lifetime. Of all the incidents mentioned in our history book, one in particular captured my fancy. It was the story of Ponce De Leon. De Leon was a Spaniard, as I remember it. He was one of the adventurous souls that accompanied Columbus to America. He had heard the natives speaking, in glowing terms, of a remarkable stream of water called the Fountain of Youth. According to the Indians, anyone who was fortunate enough to drink this wonderful water would never grow old. In view of the stories from Eastern Asia that were prevalent at that time about a similar kind of a spring, you could hardly blame the Spaniard for getting excited about the prospect of discovering this miraculous fountain. Why, his fortune was assured, if he could but bottle up some of the water and take it back to Europe! What king would not offer half of his fortune for such a boon! So De Leon set out in search of the Fountain of Youth. We know from history that he never succeeded in finding it, although he did discover what we know today as the state of Florida.

The thought that captured my boyish imagination then, and even more now, is: Wouldn't it be grand to have the joys that cling only to youth, and, at the same time, the wisdom and the experience that come only with age? What a glorious thought: to be eternally youthful! As a matter of fact, we know that in God's ordinary providence, we must all grow older and eventually die. That's part of the punishment for the sin of our first parents.

But there is a still greater and more unbelievable Fountain of Youth than the one that attracted Ponce De Leon. We don't believe in the existence of this one on the word of a group of credulous savages, or even because of the honeyed phrases of some smooth-selling business promoter. We have it on the word of God Himself. Our Fountain of Youth is Holy Communion. Jesus Christ Himself has said, "If anyone eats my flesh, or drinks my blood, He shall not taste death forever." And that is precisely what happens when we receive Holy Communion; we receive the flesh and blood of Christ Himself, under the appearance of bread.

There are many other great benefits that stem from the reception of Holy Communion. Every Communion we receive strengthens our souls against temptation. No matter how zealously we may strive to avoid the occasions of sin, we will never be able to completely avoid temptation. Like "flu" germs, during an epidemic, temptations are everywhere. We can do one thing, however, and that is strengthen our resistance. That is precisely what Holy Communion accomplishes for our souls.

Perhaps some of us have more than temptations to deal with; perhaps we have already contracted bad habits. In that case, we need the help of Communion even more. Just as there are certain physical diseases that can be successfully combated only through the medium of a blood transfusion, there are certain spiritual diseases that can be conquered only by a divine blood transfusion. A worthy Communion is like a blood transfusion.

Every Holy Communion brings us into the closest possible contact with the keenest thinker, the most sympathetic adviser, the most powerful friend, and the most magnetic personality the world has ever known!

In addition to all these evident advantages of Holy Communion, there are many, many others. For example, every Holy Communion cuts down the amount of suffering that awaits me in purgatory. Offhand, that may not sound like such a tremendous inducement, but only if we have the wrong idea of purgatory. It is not a mere waiting room for the Heavenly Express, a place where we park and mark time, while we're waiting for the Lord to post our number. Purgatory is a place of intense suffering. In fact, some of our great Catholic teachers have declared that the only essential difference between the pains of hell and the pains of purgatory is the fact that the pains of purgatory will not last forever. Evidently, therefore, anything that will shorten our stay in purgatory is worth while.

Every Holy Communion adds a definite degree to the happiness that will be yours in heaven. Due to no fault of your own, many of you may never have the pleasure of living in a beautiful home on this earth, but there is absolutely no reason why you can't bank on a high place in heaven, if you go to Holy Communion often.

Why is it that, despite the almost unbelievable premiums attached to frequent Holy Communion, so few people receive with any degree of regularity? Why has the altar rail become a fence that separates so many people from the altar, instead of the heavenly table that the Church intends it to be? If people make a sacrifice of their time to offer up a gift to God, which is the Mass, why don't they take advantage of their presence at Mass, and receive Holy Communion which is God's gift to them? You wouldn't go to a banquet and listen to all the speeches, and then not eat any of the food that is served. You wouldn't pay an exorbitant amount for a ticket to some "prom" and not dance, would you? You wouldn't go to the beach on a warm day and not go in the water, would you? Then why, for heaven's sake — and I mean that expression literally — do you make a sacrifice of your time to go to Mass, and then not take advantage there of your presence and God's generosity and receive Holy Communion?

You hear many excuses for failure to receive Holy Communion frequently. Frequently means every Sunday when you're at Mass. Of course, the ideal would be daily Communion; but what's the use of talking about daily Communion, if you don't even go weekly? Here are a few of the alibis.

"I'd go to Holy Communion oftener, but Sunday is the only day I've got to sleep. I'm out late on Saturday night, and so I go to a late Mass on Sunday. No one goes to Communion at that Mass."

I don't blame you for sleeping late on Sunday morning. If I were a Catholic layman, you'd probably find me at a late Mass, too. But why can't you go to Communion at the late Mass? Suppose you do have to quit eating at midnight — isn't it worth a little sacrifice to receive our Lord into your heart? Surely our Lord means more to you than a "coke" and a hamburger!

"But if I go to Holy Communion at the late Mass, I get a headache."

Isn't it worth a little discomfort, when you consider how much our Lord does for you? Too often the very ones who complain about the sacrifice in getting to Communion on Sunday are the same ones who would diet for a month to lose a couple of pounds, or who would get up in the early hours of the morning to go on a hunting or fishing trip, or to play golf or tennis.

"Well, to be honest with you, Father, it isn't the fasting that bothers me so much — it's the nuisance of having to go to Confession every Saturday night."

Who in the world ever said that you *had to* go to Confession before every Holy Communion? The Catholic Church certainly doesn't say so. The only time you're *bound* to go to Confession, before receiving Holy Communion, is when you are absolutely certain that you are in the state of mortal sin. Otherwise, all you need is a good act of contrition.

"But Father, I wouldn't feel right if I went to Communion without going to Confession first. I'd feel funny."

Feel funny, but go to Holy Communion anyway. That's the only way you're ever going to get over that "queer" feeling. There is no reason why you should put yourself up on a pedestal, why it should be any more difficult for you to receive Holy Communion than it is for anyone else.

"Gosh, Father, I go to Communion every month? What do you want me to be, a saint?"

It must be nice to feel that you don't need the help of our Blessed Lord, as much as the Pope, bishops, priests, sisters, and good lay people, who receive Holy Communion every day, not because they are saints, but because they realize how much they need the help of our Lord. And don't forget, a good many of those mentioned are not exposed to nearly as many temptations as you are.

"My case is different, though. Everyone in our parish knows me, and they know that I'm no saint. If I went up to the Communion rail every Sunday, I'm sure that they would all think I was trying to show off. They'd probably be thinking to themselves: Look at the hypocrite. Why doesn't she stay in the pew, where she belongs?"

Well, the peculiar part of it all is that the real "grandstanders" and "show offs" in church on Sunday morning are not the ones who march up to the Communion rail but the ones who remain in the pew. Here's why. When you receive Holy Communion you are saying equivalently, for everyone in the Church to understand: "I need the help of Christ; I can't get along without Him!" But what are you saying, if you don't go up to Communion? Simply this: "I get along without You very well."

There is one excuse that irritates most of all. When you have answered every possible objection, somebody always comes up with this one.

"Father, I'd go to Holy Communion oftener, but I don't think that I'm worthy." Then they bow their head very humbly, and flutter their eyelashes very coyly, and you're supposed to think: "My goodness, doesn't she look just like the Little Flower — or isn't he a dead "ringer" for St. Aloysius!" If they only knew what you were actually thinking. . . .

Holy Communion was not meant as a reward for worthiness; it was meant as a help for weakness. The worse we are, the more we need the help of our Blessed Lord. Actually if Holy Communion were only given to those who are worthy, there never would have been a single Holy Communion distributed in the history of the Catholic Church, and that includes our Blessed Mother herself. After all, who can be *worthy of God?*

One final thought on this most important subject. Imagine that you are on the verge of that delightful period in your life called courtship. The object of your affections is very romantic and also most desirous of frequently sharing your company. In fact, after protestations of love and declarations of undying esteem, your lover asks if it would be all right to spend at least three evenings a week with you. Not to be outdone in any way by the ardor of your lover's sentiments, you, of course, swear your everlasting love in tones that fairly quiver with emotion. And then you say: "You can come to see me once a month, or once every three months, but you can stay only ten or fifteen minutes when you come."

Can you imagine any lover being gullible enough to fall for that? Could you blame anyone for believing that your love was nothing more than words?

Let's apply this example to our Lord. He loves you with an everlasting love. He loved you even unto His death on the cross. He loves you far more than you could possibly love yourself. He has humiliated Himself, under a veil of bread, so that you may approach

Him more easily. He begs you to take advantage of His presence in the Blessed Sacrament.

Our Blessed Lord is saying to you, right now, from the depths of the tabernacle: "If you love Me, as you claim to do in words, prove it by taking Me into your heart, at least every Sunday, when you are at Mass."

Chapter 9

OUR "SECRET WEAPON"

A FEW years ago, the entire country was stirred up by the kidnapping of the Lindbergh baby. Naturally, the newspapers, with customary disregard for the feelings of the parents, devoted column after column to playing up the unfortunate incident. One of the items they printed aroused a storm of criticism in Catholic circles. It was an interview, signed by a prominent non-Catholic minister, in which he deplored the hysteria that was gripping the country. According to him, some of the people had sunk so low that they were reverting to the instincts of primitive savages, by praying to God to help them find the baby!

Were I to question any of you regarding that minister's statement, you would very indignantly disagree with him. Were you asked a reason, you would probably quote the words, "Ask and you shall receive." "If you ask the Father *anything* in My name, He will give it to you." If our Lord thought enough of us to die on the cross for us, He certainly will not turn a deaf ear to any reasonable request of ours.

Theoretically, you all believe in the value of prayer. But do you put that belief into practice? Do you always act upon that belief? There's a world of difference, you know, between theory and practice. For example, you may be firmly convinced that there is nothing like prompt rising in the morning; but, when morning rolls around, and the bed is nice and warm, you just don't get up. Or, you may be absolutely convinced of the necessity of dieting, but the very first night of your diet, a delicious dessert is served, and your good resolutions go right out the window. It's the same with prayer. Every reader of this book would probably deny that minister's assertion about the folly of prayer, but how many are consistent enough to live their life in accordance with their belief in prayer? How many of you begin and end each day with a prayer, say your grace before and after meals, pray to our Lord not only in your sorrows, but also in your joys, pray in moments of temptation and in hours of heartache and trouble?

What's the reason for the inconsistency between what we believe and what we do about prayer?

First of all, some of us have the wrong idea of prayer. We think that it means kneeling down and pouring out our soul to God, while angels flutter softly about our prostrate form, lest they disturb our ecstatic communion with our Creator. "It might be all right for one of the saints, but what chance have I, poor John Smith or Mary Jones, to climb to such great heights? So I just give up trying."

Prayer doesn't mean that! Oh, once in a while some

great saint was carried away in rapturous prayer, but that was most extraordinary. For the ordinary person, like you and me, prayer is something much different. It takes real effort on our part to concentrate on talking to a Person whom we can neither see nor hear directly. The best definition of prayer that I have ever heard is this: "To pray is to think of God, and say a word to Him."

Because it is rather difficult to pray, your prayers needn't be long. In fact, you have a much better chance of concentrating on your prayers if they are short. Short prayers can carry terrific weight. For proof of this statement, consider the single sentence of the thief next to Christ on the cross. He was the equivalent of a twentieth-century racketeer, guilty of every crime in the book, getting a punishment that he richly deserved. Yet the few words, "Lord, remember me when Thou shalt come into thy kingdom," won eternal salvation for him.

You needn't use a prayer book, either. In fact, you're sometimes better off, if you get along without one. A prayer book is like a crutch. If you can't get along any other way, then use it. After all, a prayer book contains a lot of "canned prayers." Very often the prayers you recite do not express your true feelings. For example, you may come back from Communion, pick up your prayer book and start reading, "Oh, God, my heart is a burning furnace of charity, etc." All the while, your heart may be as cold as a landlord's. Can you imagine expressing your love to the "one and only" out of a book? Or again, you may read a prayer like, "Oh, Thou ineffable fount of love, vouchsafe to grant me, etc." Can you imagine asking your friends for anything in words like that? Isn't it much better to talk to the Lord "straight from the shoulder," in your own language? You'll get a lot farther that way. It's all right to use a prayer book occasionally, for certain beautiful prayers, or if that is the only way you can keep your mind on what you're doing. But try to avoid being a mere *reader* of prayers.

Another reason why we're not consistent in our attitude toward prayer is our own carelessness and laziness. We roll out of bed in the morning and, if we think of our prayers, we dismiss them by saying to ourselves, "Oh, I'll say them on the way down to work, or later in the day." But something generally manages to turn up, and we end up by not saying them at all. On the other hand, we may not have the slightest intention of saying our prayers. We're just downright lazy. We console ourselves by thinking that it's not a sin to omit our prayers — at least, it's not a mortal sin. That is absolutely true — it is not a sin to skip your night and morning prayers. It isn't a sin to skip a shave, or to go without "makeup," either. But how many of you would dream of advancing such an excuse for neglecting either one of those things?

It's the same with grace before and after meals. Just because it is not a sin to omit grace, there is no reason for skipping it. How many of you would ever dare to leave a dinner party, where you had been a guest, without thanking the host or hostess? No matter how bored you may have been all evening, at the time when you can gracefully leave, you call upon your reserve strength, summon up a sickly smile, and then turn to the hostess, and say, "I want to thank you for a perfectly lovely evening!" If you can do that, simply to obey the dictates of polite society — for it is a sign of good breeding to show your gratitude for a favor — why can't you do it, when it comes to thanking God, to whom you are indebted, not only for the food you eat, but for your very existence? You can't avoid the issue by saying, "But I can never remember the words for grace." Words are not essential. If you simply bow your head, before and after you have your meal, and say, "Thanks, Lord," you've said a splendid grace. You know, one of the primary meanings of the word grace is thanks!

While on this subject of prayer, a few words should be said about the discouraging thought of prayers that go unanswered. But, there is no such thing as an unanswered prayer! "Is that so?" you are saying to yourself. "Well, I've had plenty of prayers that were not answered." No — the truth is, you always got some kind of an answer, but it might not have been the answer that you wanted. All of which, of course, brings up the question — why? Why didn't you always get what you asked for?

There are a number of reasons for that. Perhaps you didn't pray hard enough; perhaps you didn't pray long enough; maybe what you asked for was not for your own good.

Before the war, a lady whom I visited had a son away at college, studying to be a lawyer. Naturally, in the course of our conversation, I asked her how her son Bill was doing at school. Her answer was, "Oh, it's the same old story, Father. He takes it easy all semester, and when exam time comes around, he becomes very religious, and makes a novena for success in his studies."

Could you blame our Lord if he let Bill flunk? It isn't right to put Him "on the spot" that way. We ought to work as though everything depended on ourselves, and pray as though everything depended on God. In other words, we've got to do our share, if we expect our Lord to do His.

Let the Lord be the final judge of what is best for us. Very often, in our short-sightedness, because we are blinded by the glamour of this passing world, we ask for things that would eventually prove very harmful to our souls. So God gives us, not what we ask for, but something else instead. A mother may think the world of her infant son, and yet, no matter how loudly or piteously he cries for the carving knife, she will not give it to him. Instead, she gives him a rattle to play with. Not because she doesn't love that child, but because she does love him, and she knows that the knife would cut him. We're children in God's eyes, you know, and He takes the same good care of us.

Be grateful for the answers to your prayers that our Lord does give you. Don't be like the newsboy in the story that follows.

A very wealthy and charitable lady once hit upon the idea of serving a turkey dinner, on Christmas Day, to all the paper boys in New York City. The large hall she hired for the occasion was jammed to the doors, and all the boys did full justice to the meal. As she walked around the banquet tables, the kind-hearted lady noticed one little boy who seemed to be enjoying the meal more than any of his neighbors, judging from the almost unbelievable amount of food he consumed. He ate, and ate, and ate, until the good lady figured that he must not have had a solid meal in weeks. When the dessert time came, she decided to have the pleasure of serving him herself, and so she selected a huge piece of apple pie and placed it before him. Imagine her amazement when the little fellow looked up at her and said, "What! No cheese, lady?"

A good many of us are like that newsboy. Our dear Lord gives us a good home, wonderful parents, splendid health, and all kinds of other gifts that we don't even realize. And what do we do? We look up at our Lord, and, instead of thanking Him from the bottom of our heart, we say, "What! No big job, Lord?" or "What! You expect me to carry a cross?"

A final word now, on distractions in prayer. If you

do not *deliberately* allow your mind to wander while you're praying, you have nothing to worry about. None of us can concentrate on prayer, without some other thoughts straying into our minds. We're creatures composed of body and soul, not just a soul. We're not machines. But to freely and deliberately allow your mind to wander is another story. It would be somewhat similar to getting a personal interview with the President of the United States. You're ushered into his private office where he sits at his desk, waiting to talk to you. But you proceed to spend your time looking at the various autographed pictures on his office wall. Believe me, your interview with him would terminate very abruptly. And rightly so. Yet, when you pray, you're having the privilege of a private interview with the King of kings. Don't you think He deserves at least as much consideration as our President?

On the other hand, don't be upset if you can't get any sweetness or spiritual consolation out of your prayers. Prayer of its very nature is difficult. That's why our Lord rewards us for our efforts. The dryer and more difficult our prayer, the more value it probably has in the sight of God, because we're thinking of Him, and not of ourselves. If it were easy to pray, would there be any special prize for it? If it were easy to pray, you'd have to barricade the churches to keep the people out!

Let me sum up the entire idea of prayer in a couple of sentences. God puts us on this earth to serve Him, and through that service, save our souls for the ever-lasting joys of heaven. But it is not always easy to serve God. Very often, it becomes extremely difficult. We need every help that we can get, along the rocky road to heaven. We'd certainly be foolish, if we deliberately neglected any help that is offered. One of our biggest helps is prayer. It is one of the greatest sources of strength that God has placed at our disposal. Don't fail to make use of it. If you do, you'll regret it. Take the advice of Christ, our Lord, who said, "Watch and pray, lest ye enter into temptation."

PURCELL HIGH SCHOOL LIBRARY
2935 HACKBERRY STREET
CINCINNATI 6, OHIO

Chapter 10

INDIAN GIVER

IN THE language of the neighborhood where I was born, an "Indian giver" was a person who gave you something and, later on, demanded it back. Naturally, "Indian givers" were most unpopular, especially if they were powerful enough to enforce their request. However, there is one "Indian giver" who has every right to ask that His gifts be given back — that "Indian Giver" is Almighty God.

God gave us our lives; and He requires that we freely surrender them to Him, in some way or other, under penalty of being separated from Him forever after death. We may give our lives back to God either in the single, the religious, or the married state, or as a widow or widower — just as we may serve our country either as a civilian, or as a soldier, sailor, or marine. We may be volunteers in our state of life (religious or married life) or we may be draftees (single or widowed people). The armed forces have their heroes and their cowards, their good fighters and their poor ones; so, too, there are heroes and cowards in every walk of life. Many a brave member of our armed forces fought and died without praise. And there are many uncrowned saints in the battle of life, who will receive their just recognition only from their Supreme Commander and Chief after death.

What is the highest state in life? Logically, you are expected to say that the religious life is the most perfect, because there is in it less consideration of self and more consideration for others, out of love for God. That is the logical and true answer. But, practically speaking, any one of the various states of life may be the highest for a particular individual, depending upon his or her personal motives and the manner in which the life is lived. Any state of life in which a person becomes a saint must be a perfect state of life for that person.

All the states in life have one thing in common; they require genuine sacrifice upon our part if they are to be lived intelligently. There must be some sacrifice in the vocation that we choose, and we must be willing to accept that sacrifice. Where there is no sacrifice, there is no love; where there is no love, there will be no heaven. The sacrifices of the married, religious, and widowed life are apparent. The sacrifice of the single life involves the inevitable loneliness of an unmarried person, together with a denial of all sexual pleasures, and the difficulties that spring from performing works of charity.

This is no attempt to "sell" anyone on a certain vocation. That is a choice each person makes for himself. But a few observations on the various states of life, gathered from books on the subject and from the experience of a curate and a missionary, may be a practical guide in the prayerful selection of your state in life.

To begin with the single state of life, there are *volunteers* and there are *draftees* among single persons. Some prefer to remain single because they have no genuine attraction toward any other state in life, but this number constitutes a very small percentage of the unmarried people in the world. There are others who are too selfish and too self-centered to make the sacrifices demanded in the other states in life. There are far too many of these.

Many remain single through no wish of their own. They are attracted to the married state, or to the religious state, but there is no chance for them to realize their desire, because of their poor health, or their lack of ability, or their home conditions, or some other insuperable obstacle. Still others are drawn toward the married life but cannot find the kind of partner with whom they believe they could make a success of marriage, and so they're smart enough to remain single. Last of all comes the unfortunate person who can't get any kind of a partner.

Men and women who deliberately choose the single life because it involves the least sacrifice will certainly receive the least reward from Almighty God. On the other hand, those who freely give up their chance to enter married or religious life, in order to raise their younger brothers or sisters, or to provide for their aging parents, will receive probably the greatest reward of all, because they have made the greatest sacrifice. They have neither the sexual satisfactions of married life nor the spiritual consolation of religious community life. One of the saintliest women I have ever known was one who gave up her desire to become a nun, so that she might care for her aged mother.

You, who may choose to spend your life in the single state, learn now to make a personal companion of our Blessed Lord through frequent Holy Communion and daily prayer. Then, when moments of loneliness come into your life — moments that are bound to come — you can fall back upon Him for companionship. When temptations against purity besiege you — and they will — you can cling to Him for strength. Never forget that, regardless of your state in life, if you have Christ our Lord with you, you have everything. If He is not with you, you have nothing.

Most of you, however, are much more concerned with marriage. Since the day in the Garden of Eden when Almighty God said to Adam, "It is not good for a man to be alone," men and women have experienced the urge to enter into the matrimonial state. You, who are considering it, must be impressed right away with the fact that it is a mighty serious proposition, the most serious, perhaps, that you will be called upon to face in your whole life. Your happiness on this earth and your eternal salvation depend, to a very great extent, upon the kind of person whom you marry. For the sake of your own immortal soul, and the souls that may be entrusted to your care, don't overlook a single point, in making your decision. It is true that every marriage involves a certain amount of risk. No one can lay down rules that are absolutely guaranteed for making a perfect choice of a life partner. But it does lie within your power to cut down the odds against you, by taking advantage of the practical advice of your mother and dad, sermons that you've heard, and books that you've read. Above all, pray for divine guidance and help. Your unborn children are pleading with you, right now, to choose the kind of partner who will assure them a happy home.

Sometimes it happens that young men and women get the idea that marriage is a career for weaklings. If you're not brave enough, or unselfish enough, to enter religious life, they say, you can always "get by" in married life. When the word "vocation" is mentioned, they always associate it with the religious life. What a travesty on the truth that is! Marriage is one of the four great vocations. It is a grand, glorious, and difficult state of life, one that requires the constant practice of the highest virtues.

The Church depends upon splendid mothers and fathers for the fostering of religious vocations. One fine Catholic girl remarked to me, when we were discussing her vocation, "Father, I've decided to get married and raise a family, because I think the world needs good Catholic mothers right now, more than it needs good nuns." Next to Almighty God and His grace, I believe I owe my religious vocation to the magnificent example of my saintly mother.

But, getting back to a few "pointers" on the selection of a spouse: First, don't marry for "looks." He may look like Robert Taylor, in his evening clothes, or like an all-American, in his football outfit, but his character is going to make or break your marriage. She may be "gorgeous" in a "formal," but how will she be when she has to sit up all night with a sick baby? Many a man married what he considered to be a "dream girl," only to discover after a few years of married life that she was nothing but a "nightmare." If good looks are your future partner's only recommendation, then, when they fade, you're going to have only memories, to help you bear the difficulties of your state in life, and memories will not be enough. You needn't go out looking for a "gargoyle" or a "Frankenstein," but you'll probably be much better off if your lovemate is not a Clark Gable or a Betty Grable in appearance. Then, you probably won't have to worry so much about your spouse.

Second, *don't marry a non-Catholic, or a careless Catholic.* The reason for this is not that Catholics are better than non-Catholics — only too often does it happen that just the contrary is true. Some of the finest people that I have ever met have been non-Catholics. But religion is the most fundamental thing in our lives, because it determines our relationship toward Almighty God, our Creator. The least a married couple can do is start their common life in agreement on the fundamentals. The Lord knows that they will find enough accidentals to disagree upon. Your religion will demand sacrifices of you that your non-Catholic partner may not be willing to make. To mention but a few, there is the question of being married in the presence of a Catholic priest, of having your children baptized in the Catholic Church, of sending your children to a Catholic school. Then, sooner or later, you are faced with the problem of birth control.

You may, in your defense of a mixed marriage, point to certain ones that have proved successful. Granting this, the odds are still against you. Experience shows that the majority of mixed marriages have turned out poorly. Why take a chance? As for choosing a careless Catholic, except in unusual circumstances a sincere non-Catholic is a more likely choice — he, at least, is living up to his conscience.

The Catholic Church will not refuse to sanction a mixed marriage, but she does emphasize the difficulties connected with one. If, despite her warning, you choose a non-Catholic, the Church tries to safeguard your marriage by *insisting* that the non-Catholic party make certain solemn promises regarding you and your children. She then allows the ceremony to be performed, and hopes for the best.

The third rule to be followed in your effort to make

a successful marriage is this: marry someone whom you can *respect*. If your boy friend is the type that demands "liberties," which you have no right to grant, you can save yourself a lifetime of grief by breaking up with him now, no matter what kind of a "line" he gives you, for his lack of control. And if your girl friend is the kind that is free with her caresses and does not positively demand that you respect her purity, don't be a fool and take her off the market. Let some one else get "stuck" with her. The basis of all true love is self-respect. Unless you learn now, by prayerful self-control, to respect each other, you will never experience the joy of true love.

One final word, with regard to a very important pre-requisite for marriage, and that is courtship. Courtship is the period of time that immediately precedes your marriage. It is a period fraught with dangers, which you must obviate and make remote by your prayers, by frequent Communion, and by use of good common sense. There are two extremes to be avoided: getting married too quickly, and being engaged too long!

If you're in too much of a hurry to plunge into the sea of matrimonial bliss, your theme song on your first anniversary may be, "If I knew then, what I know now." "Love at first sight" marriages may go all right in the "movies," or in novels, but in real life — how often do they succeed? That may be the reason why many Hollywood marriages are such a pitiful joke.

On the other hand, there is real danger involved in

a long engagement. Familiarity, begotten by a long courtship, can very easily lead to contempt of God's laws. The pagan world allows liberties to engaged couples that Almighty God does not tolerate. People who are engaged have no more right to pleasures connected with sex than any other single person. Don't project your courtship over too long a period. Except in very unusual circumstances, from six months to a year should be plenty of time for your engagement. Incidentally, don't waste the best years of your life, waiting for a big salary. You're far better off, starting with just a little.

It should be perfectly obvious that you needn't be ashamed to pray for a good husband or wife. If, as the Church maintains, your happiness on this earth and your eternal salvation are bound up most intimately with your life partner, then you can't pray too much for guidance in selecting one. If they're worth living with, they're worth praying for. Ask our Blessed Lady, good St. Ann, and St. Joseph to help you pick a "winner."

Speaking of "picking a winner" naturally brings up the thought of the religious vocation, for what greater "winner" could anyone choose than our Blessed Lord Himself! Religious vocations are generally mentioned during a time of retreat, but very often this great state of life is misunderstood.

Sometimes, even Catholics have weird ideas on this subject. If they happen to meet a priest, let us say, informally, on a golf course, they look upon him as some kind of "freak." "Oh, are you a priest?" they will exclaim, in much the same way as they might say, "Oh, have you really got two heads?" And when they meet a Brother, many people are absolutely baffled.

The blame for this strange ignorance about the religious life should be shared by non-Catholics, Catholics, and religious themselves. Non-Catholics are at fault when they make no effort to try to understand the religious life. Some just think we're "queer," and let it go at that. Many Catholics, who haven't the faintest idea of what it is all about, think that priests and nuns are persons born with a prayer book in one hand and a string of beads in the other, who, as they grew older, experienced absolutely no attraction toward the pleasures of the world or the companionship of the opposite sex. And so the Church, with her usual ingenuity, devised a state in life, for these unusual characters. No wonder the Crosby movie, "Going My Way," was so popular. Millions of people discovered, for the first time, that priests were genuine human beings. Sometimes, religious themselves are to blame for the extraordinary misconceptions that abound with regard to the religious life. After meeting or talking with some of them, you are almost ready to believe anything that is said about their eccentricities.

It is true that a religious vocation comes from God. But that does not mean that there need be anything mysterious about it. As a matter of fact, every gift and talent we have comes from God. Nor does God communicate this gift to us in any mysterious fashion. Once in a while He did make His will known to some great saint in an extraordinary manner, but the rank and file religious has never heard any whisperings in his ear. How, then, can a person know whether he or she has a religious vocation?

It is one thing to have the qualifications for a religious life. It is another thing to accept a vocation. No one is bound to enter religious life, regardless of talents, unless he or she is *absolutely* convinced that that is the only way to save his or her soul. You can serve God well, and save your soul, without being a religious.

The ordinary signs of a religious vocation, according to all those who have made a study of this life, are rather simple.

First, there is a sincere attraction toward that kind of life. Of course, the desire to become a religious is not a conclusive sign that you have a vocation, just as the desire to become an opera singer, or a "big league" pitcher, or a doctor, or a nurse, is not enough — you must have the talents that go with the job. But the desire is one of the most important and necessary prerequisites. No one in his right senses should go into a state of life that is not attractive to him.

In addition to the desire for religious life, you must possess health that is sufficient for the type of work you will be given to do. In other words, you must be able to pass an ordinary physical examination. The reason for this requirement is very evident. Religious life is not supposed to be a rest cure for semi-invalids, but a place of good, hard work for the Lord.

Next, is the requirement of ordinary intelligence, the kind that will be necessary for doing successfully the work you will be called upon to do. The emphasis is on the word "ordinary." You needn't be a genius, but to be a good religious, you need sound, common sense. That is much more important and necessary than any degree of learning. The greatest religious have not always been the most brilliant ones.

What degree of holiness is demanded of a would-be religious? Just ordinary holiness. You don't have to be the "halo" or the "ecstatic" type. You don't have to love to spend long periods in the chapel, or be always "haunting" the church. If you love our Lord enough to receive Him every Sunday in Holy Communion, you have sufficient religious material to start working on.

Above all, if you are thinking of entering the religious life, you should have an active sense of humor. Without that, you will make it very difficult for yourself and for all those around you. "From a sad religious, O Lord, deliver us!"

If you're a person who has a lot of "pep," who likes to dance and sing, who loves a good time, and who enjoys the companionship of members of the opposite sex, you would make a splendid religious, provided you were willing to make the sacrifices that go with that state of life. For you are perfectly normal, and it is the normal people who make good religious. In the years to come, you would be able to understand and guide thousands of other normal young men, women, and children who come to you for guidance and help.

Many problems may confront you, in this matter of a religious vocation. It may be a question of parental objections, or the fear that you may not be able to persevere in that life, or the advisability of entering immediately upon your religious career. There are as many difficulties as there are individuals. That is why you should have a regular confessor, and a priest or nun to go to for help. Be prepared to abide by their advice and decisions.

Every prospective religious will wonder: "How can I be sure that religious life is my vocation?" You can't be absolutely certain, but how many times in life can you be absolutely certain? You're not sure, either that you will be in love with "Romeo" or "Juliet" all your life. Yet, it's the only choice you'll ever have. You must trust God to take care of you, once you've taken the step. A would-be nun has a couple of years to investigate the religious life, at close range. A young man aspiring to the priesthood or brotherhood has many years to spend, before he is called upon to make a lasting decision. If it were half as difficult to get married as it is to enter into religious life, we would probably have far more happy marriages.

The religious life is a wonderful life, if you are willing to make the sacrifices that go with it. We have our Lord's word for that. He Himself said, "Everyone that has left house, or brethren, or sisters, or father, or mother, or wife, or children, or lands, for My name's sake, shall receive a hundredfold, and shall possess life everlasting" (Matthew 19:29).

Chapter 11

OUR HERO

ALL the world loves a hero. Whether we realize it or not, we are all hero worshipers at heart. We not only place certain people on a pedestal, but, whenever it is possible, we try to imitate them. For proof of this bold statement, just review your life from childhood days.

You girls looked up to the older girls in your neighborhood. You yearned for the day when you would be "grown-up" and could act like them. When you entered high school, or reached high-school age, the height of your ambition was to be recognized by the mighty seniors, who dominated the school's social life. Some of you strove to imitate the dashing belle of the upper class, the leader of the school "prom." Others developed a great admiration for certain nuns and began to ape their mannerisms. Perhaps you even began to keep diaries and scrap books in which you pasted the pictures of your heroes and heroines. You spent a great deal of time, too, day dreaming about how you would act in case you ever met them. By the time high-school days were behind you, these heroes faded from your memories and new ones came to take their place. You began to try to acquire the charm and the glamour of certain movie actresses, or stage stars, or leading society figures. No costume was too bizarre, no "make-up" too exotic, provided your movie heroines or fashion plates were advocating them.

Men were just as bad, if not worse, when it came to hero worship. When we were boys, there was always some fellow down the block, or in the upper grades at school, who we thought was the last word in masculine desirability. Maybe it was because he was a good marble shooter, with a lot of "steam," or because he was rumored to be able to "loop" a top until the string wore out. Maybe he could hit a base-ball a mile, do all sorts of tricks off the highest board at the swimming pool, or outdistance everyone on ice skates. When I was a caddy, at the advanced age of eleven, we all fought for the privilege of carrying the club champion's bag. The "champ" had a very peculiar putting stroke, and it was really amusing to notice all the caddies at the club using exactly the same putting style when they played.

As we grew older, we abandoned our grammar school heroes, in favor of newly found and more attractive ones. In our freshman year at high school, we fairly worshiped at the shrine of the football or basketball captain. To be seen in his company, or to have him call us by our "nicknames," was always our secret ambition. We longed for the time when we too could sport a "letter" for athletic prowess, so that we could swagger around the neighborhood and impress all the young ladies. I can remember when the goal of my life was to be able to wear a raccoon coat, like one of my sister's boy friends. I didn't care how I looked, as long as people thought I was "collegiate." The only reason I didn't sport a "crew" haircut then, was because this tonsorial nightmare was as yet undreamed of. And it's too late, now.

With high-school days behind us, a new galaxy of stars came into our hero life. We began to go around in "sweat" shirts, sloppy socks, rolled up trousers, and a lazy slouch. The more lifeless and bored we appeared in our movements, the more "collegiate" we thought we were — unless, of course, we were driving a car. Then our ambition was to imitate the lads who owned a Ford "jallopy," with all the "corny" wisecracks painted on every conceivable part of the car, and thunder around the neighboring blocks, like cowboys, terrorizing older pedestrians, and deeply impressing passing "glamour girls."

One thing, though, we boys and girls experienced in common. As we grew older, we began to view with complacency these youthful peculiarities, and to label them as juvenile failings, not to be indulged in by mature, serious-minded adults. The reason for discarding or shelving our old heroes was always the same; we discovered that they had "feet of clay." Incidentally, that is one of the saddest shocks we ever have, when we find out for the first time how human and how imperfect our heroes actually are. And yet, despite all the experience we have had in the past with shattered idols, we still continue the same old worship. The only difference is that we have new shrines. There are certain priests whom, consciously or unconsciously, I am trying to imitate. You have certain lay people in mind. Perhaps it is a prominent club woman or a successful businessman. Perhaps, and I wish this were true for practically all of you, it is some good Catholic mother or father.

In the line of sports, we're as bad as, if not worse than, we were in grammar school. At some football games you'd think you were among a group of lunatics. Why, I know a prominent businessman, the father of a large family, who traveled over two hundred miles, round trip, a few years ago, just to visit the injured star of one of Notre Dame's football teams. I can vouch for the story, because I went with him!

Why this lengthy discourse about hero worshipers and hero imitators? What's so terribly wrong about setting up a hero? There is really nothing wrong. Hero worshiping is a natural instinct, and the Catholic Church has always understood this fact. That is why, with God's help, she selects certain men and women for our admiration and imitation. The Church doesn't use the word hero, though. She calls them saints. Evidently, therefore, it would be most unwise to argue against hero worshiping as such. The trouble is that the majority of us pick the wrong heroes to imitate.

Why not look up to some one really worth while, whom you will never have to discard in time or in eternity?

Over nineteen hundred years ago, the greatest hero this world has ever seen, or ever will see, died upon a cross. Jesus Christ was a leader, before whose courage that of even the most renowned heroes pales and fades away. That may sound strange, since we generally picture Christ as the meekest of men. How could a man who said, "Learn of Me, because I am meek and humble of heart," be a dauntless hero?

The answer lies in a true analysis of bravery. It is easy enough to be courageous, when you know that the world is looking on with an approving eye. The thought of the recognition that will be ours seems to spur us on. Bravery is sometimes a natural reaction when we are suddenly face to face with a danger or an emergency that we had not foreseen. Even a cornered rat will fight! But it takes heroism, in the truest and noblest sense of the word, to do something extremely difficult, which you could easily have avoided, or for which you know you're not going to attract the slightest praise or commendation. That is precisely why Christ was the most courageous person who ever lived.

Before He fell into the clutches of His enemies, He knew exactly what He would be called upon to endure. He foresaw the heart-breaking ingratitude of the traitor apostle and newly ordained priest, Judas, who was to sell his allegiance for thirty measly pieces of silver. He saw, in the Garden of Olives, the tidal wave of sin that would engulf His soul, leave Him gasping at the stench and corruption, and cause His body to break out into a bloody sweat. He saw the insulting trial at the palace of Caiphas, the mockery of justice before Pilate. The humiliating scourging at the pillar would leave His skin hanging in shreds. The disgusting coronation ceremony in the barracks by the rough Roman soldiers and the brutal crowning with thorns would tear His sacred head wide open. He felt the utter agony of that long journey to Calvary, with a heavy cross upon His quivering back — the shame that would sweep over Him, when He was stripped of His garments in the open sight of all the crowd — the pain that would accompany this stripping, as His skin came off with the bloody clothes — the torture that would run through His body, as the heavy spikes were pounded through His hands and feet — the sorrow that would fill His heart, when He saw His dearest Mother suffering with Him beneath the cross — the thirst that would rack His parched body and His fevered lips, as the blood poured out from His veins — the terrible sense of loneliness, when He was abandoned by His Father, a loneliness that would make Him cry, "My God, My God, why hast Thou forsaken Me?" — the cowardice of His chosen apostles and friends, who would leave Him in His hour of need like frightened children — the discouraging and depressing realization that there would probably be hundreds of thousands of men and women who, through their own fault would never profit by all His sufferings.

Christ knew, too, that when He would hang on the cross, there would be no bands playing there to encourage Him. There would be no cheering crowd to spur Him on. Nothing but a flood of blasphemies and curses from a thoughtless, senseless mob.

Christ foresaw all those sufferings clearly and, remember, He did not have to undergo them. One single sigh, one tiny drop of His precious blood, would have been more than sufficient to redeem the world. Yet He freely suffered it all, out of love for us, and to be for all of us the perfect model of courage.

Life will call upon you to make many sacrifices in the name of your religion. The road to heaven will not be a "waltz" for any of you. Right now it is the question of personal purity. Later on it may be the problem of birth control, or the necessity of denying yourself so that your children may receive a Catholic education. It may be the dragon of drink, or the great god of money, or, perhaps, your desire for social prominence that will clash with your religious beliefs. Of one thing you may be certain, Almighty God will ask you for something difficult to prove your love. Whatever price He may ask, let the example of Christ spur you on. Here is a true hero to worship and imitate, in the sufferings that are bound to come into the lives of all of us, or that may have come already.

The one great purpose of this life is to serve your God and Maker. Now you have an ideal, something to aim at, something that will spur you on, when the going is tough. They say that, down at Notre Dame, when the coach had resorted to every other means without success, he could always key his men to a fighting pitch, by saying, "Let's win this one for Rockne." Why can't we do the same thing in our lives? When we're face to face with a serious decision, or we're up against a difficult temptation, let's say to ourselves, "I'm going to win this one for Christ!"

The example of Christ helped to spur all the saints on to the very heights of heaven. See what it did for the great convert, St. Paul.

As a young man, Paul, or Saul, as he was then known, had opposed the Catholic religion very bitterly. He had actually demanded and received letters from the high priest at Jerusalem, authorizing him to attack the Christians at Damascus. On the road to Damascus, a strange thing happened. As he was riding along, a heavenly light struck him to the ground, and he heard a voice saying, "Saul, Saul, why persecutest thou Me? I am Jesus whom thou persecutest. It is hard for thee to kick against the goad."

That was enough for Paul. No pussy-footing, half-way measures for him. He had persecuted Christ and His followers with all his might; now he would follow Christ until death. And so he became the firebrand of God, the gamest fighter the Church has ever known.

Nothing could stop him, as he pressed on with the vision of Christ, his hero, ever before his eyes. According to his own testimony, he was scourged five different times, with thirty-nine lashes each time. Three times he was cruelly beaten with rods. Once he was stoned. Three times he was shipwrecked. Time after time he exposed himself to the violence of mobs. Near the end of his life, they put him in chains in Rome, and finally beheaded him. As he was awaiting his execution, he certainly could have said what he often said before, "I live now, not I, but Christ liveth in me." He had followed and studied Christ, his hero, so closely that he had become Christlike.

It may be true that God does not give every one of us the grace to be a St. Paul, but He does place before all of us the example of His divine Son. The more closely we succeed in imitating Him, the greater will be our reward in heaven. Let's beg Him, with all the fervor at our command, to always be our hero. Let's ask Him to give us the grace to know Him more intimately, to follow Him more closely, and to love Him more deeply. Then, we may be able to repeat with all sincerity, the beautiful words of this poem, called *Rabboni*:

"When I am dying, how glad I shall be
  That the lamp of my life, has been burned out
    for Thee.
That sorrow has darkened the pathway I trod;
That thorns, not roses, were strewn o'er its sod.

That anguish of spirit full often was mine,
Since anguish of spirit so often was Thine.
My cherished Rabboni, how glad I shall be,
To die with the hope of a welcome from Thee."

Chapter 12

A POSTSCRIPT FOR PARENTS

THIS book was written primarily for single, young people, but the author hopes that it will be read also by their parents. That is the reason for this postscript.

When it comes to dealing with their children, too many parents are conscious of their rights and unconscious of their duties. It is unquestionably true that parents have a solemn right, based upon the law of Almighty God Himself, to demand love, reverence, and obedience from their children. Mothers and fathers never let their children forget it. They always insist upon it. They are deeply hurt when they do not receive it. But how many parents are equally careful when it comes to shouldering their responsibilities toward their children? It is most important that parents understand their obligations toward their offspring. Many of the young men and women who are making a wreck out of their lives are suffering, to a very great extent, from the failure of their parents to fulfill their obligations toward them.

The first duty is that of example. If you fail to practice what you preach, you might just as well quit preaching. If you tell your son not to drink, and come home drunk yourself; if you tell your daughter not to listen to smutty stories, and tell them yourself; if you tell your son or daughter not to go to certain types of amusement, and go yourself — then you are nothing but a hypocrite! And no one ever pays much attention to what a hypocrite says.

You cannot expect your children to attend Mass regularly, to receive our Lord in Communion frequently, and to be present at parochial devotions, if you do not give them the example. They may go while they are "under your thumb," and are forced to go, but as soon as they are able, they're going to start "ducking," unless they have a far better character than their folks have. You may fool your children once in a while, but they'll "catch on" to you, soon or later.

Give your home a religious atmosphere. Have a few religious objects, not hidden away in the dim recesses of your bedroom, but in the broad daylight of the living room. Say the rosary (or part of it) together, every now and then. You'll be surprised how it draws the family together, and promotes real love and happy memories. I can remember how we used to say the rosary in our home, every evening during Lent. There were eleven of us, counting my mother and father, and we would take turns leading the decades. Naturally, among the younger members of the family, there was giggling and snickering every now and then, but it wasn't mother's or father's fault!

The second duty of parents toward their children is that of being firm in their dealings with them. Try to avoid the extremes of harshness and softness. When you are too strict, it's really a form of tyranny. Such cruelty soon or later causes rebellion, and destroys your children's love for you. Don't always be giving orders, and use physical punishment only as a last resort. It's really difficult to love a person who hurts you. On the other hand, don't be too easygoing. Giving in to a son or daughter's whims and fancies is a mistaken idea of kindness. The surest way to spoil young people is to give them their own way all the time. Don't molly-coddle them, because it will make their characters weak and selfish. The inspired writer spoke with the wisdom of the ages when he said, "Spare the rod and spoil the child." Above all, never deal with your children if you have lost your temper. Wait until you have cooled down. If you really think the matter deserves physical punishment, say a prayer first.

Third, let your language be beyond reproach at all times. How it saddens a person to meet young people who have contracted the habit of using profane and even obscene language from their own parents! When such parents are questioned, their only defense is, "Well, I told them not to use those nasty words."

Fourth, if you drink liquor, be moderate in its use. Almighty God does not begrudge you the pleasure that comes from liquor, if you use it moderately and on the proper occasion. But if you should ever have the misfortune, through human weakness, of indulging too much, in the name of all the angels and saints, don't let your children see or hear you in that condition. Young people will never forget a thing like that.

Fifth, keep an eye on your children's recreation. Make it your business to find out whom they are "going around" with. If you don't like their choice of companions, tell them so, and explain what you find undesirable in them. If there is some serious defect of character in their associates, use your parental authority and, as a last resort, forbid your children to keep company with them.

Throw your home open to your sons' and daughters' friends. Let them feel that they are always welcome to get the "gang" together at your house, where they can have some clean, wholesome fun. This may cause you considerable inconvenience at times, but it's a great deal easier to mend a broken davenport, or buy a new rug, than it is to mend a broken heart. And in the long run, it's going to save you a lot of worry. God wants young people to enjoy themselves — whether you like it or not, they are going to go around in groups. So you might just as well make the best of the situation. Your youngsters are a great deal safer in your parlor, or basement, than in some cocktail lounge, or cheap dance hall.

One final word about education. If it is humanly possible, see that your children receive a Catholic one. There can be no excuse for failing to provide your children with at least a grammar school training when there is a Catholic school in your vicinity. If you honestly feel that you cannot afford a Catholic grammar school, go to see your pastor or the Sister superior. If you are deserving, your children will receive free tuition. If they do not, and it is not through lack of sacrifice upon your part, then, before God, you will not be responsible. On the other hand, any parents who, through selfishness or because they want their children to make the proper worldly connections, send their son or daughter to a non-Catholic school, will have a serious accounting to make to Almighty God. This is not a blanket condemnation of Catholics in non-Catholic high schools and colleges, but if the cap fits, you must wear it.

All these things are difficult to put into practice, but the results are well worth the effort. Not only will God reward you on judgment day for a job well done, but you will reap the harvest even in this life. Your children will love, reverence, and obey you. You will be a model and an inspiration to them in their own lives. One of the greatest blessings God can give to any boy or girl is good Catholic parents.

4369